BODENSEE PANORAMA

© All photographs
Holger Spiering & Edition Panorama

© All texts
Iris Lemanczyk & Edition Panorama

© Captions
Holger Spiering & Edition Panorama

ISBN: 978-3-89823-415-3

Concept: Holger Spiering & Sebastian Wipfler
Design: Marcus Bela Schmitt / Designgruppe Fanz und Neumayer
Translations: Global-Text Fachübersetzungen, Heidelberg | Mark Woolfe
Editorial Department: Wolf Roth, Dr. Michael Barchet, Dr. Christophe Klimmer
Separations: Holger Spiering & EPS GmbH, Speyer
Printing: Passavia Druckservice GmbH & Co. KG, Passau
Bookbinding: Buchbinderei Terbeck, Coesfeld

Edition Panorama GmbH
G7, 14
68159 Mannheim

www.editionpanorama.com

A production by EDITION**PANORAMA**

EDITION**PANORAMA**

Bodensee Panorama

Holger Spiering

mit Texten von Iris Lemanczyk

HOLGER SPIERING

Holger Spiering wurde 1967 in Überlingen am Bodensee geboren. Nach Abitur und Zivildienst nahm er 1989 im nordschwedischen Umeå ein Studium der Forstwissenschaft auf, das er 1995 mit einem Master of Science in Forestry abschloss. Es folgten mehrere ausgedehnte Reisen nach Mittel- und Südamerika, Asien sowie Australien und Neuseeland. 1997 kehrte Holger Spiering an den Bodensee zurück, wo er seitdem mit seiner Familie lebt. *Holger Spiering was born in 1967 in Überlingen on Lake Constance. After obtaining his school-leaving certificate and completing his civilian service, he started a course of study in forestry in 1989 in Umeå in the north of Sweden, which he completed in 1995 with a Master of Science degree in forestry. This was followed by several extended trips to Central and South America, Asia, Australia and New Zealand. In 1997, Holger Spiering returned to Lake Constance, where he has since lived with his family.*

Schon während seines Studiums, besonders aber auf seinen Reisen widmete er sich intensiv seinem damaligen Hobby, der Natur- und Landschaftsfotografie und 1997 beschloss er, dieses Hobby zum Beruf zu machen. Eine Teilzeitbeschäftigung in einem Überlinger Fotogeschäft diente ihm als Einstieg. Daneben erkundete Holger Spiering im Auftrag eines großen Ansichtskartenverlags intensiv die heimatliche Bodenseelandschaft. Fotoexkursionen führten ihn ins Allgäu, die Ostschweiz und den Schwarzwald. Dazu kamen Postkartenserien, wie etwa von der Blumeninsel Mainau, die Beteiligung an Bildbänden, Reiseführern und Kalendern, sowie die Zusammenarbeit mit verschiedenen Büros für Grafikdesign. Im Sommer 2005 gründete er schließlich die Firma „Landschaftsfotografie Holger Spiering". *During his studies, and especially on his travels, he devoted himself intensely to nature and landscape photography, which was only a hobby at that time, before deciding in 1997 to make this hobby into a career. He started by taking up part-time employment in a photographic shop in Überlingen. On behalf of a large picture postcard producer, Holger Spiering also explored the landscape of Lake Constance thoroughly. Photo excursions took him to the Allgäu, eastern Switzerland and the Black Forest. This was followed by postcard series, such as on the garden island of Mainau, participation in illustrated volumes, travel guides and calendars, and cooperation with several graphic design agencies. In summer 2005 he finally founded his company "Landschaftsfotografie Holger Spiering".*

Seit 1999 widmet sich Holger Spiering besonders der Panoramafotografie, für die er zwei Fuji-Mittelformatkameras im seltenen 6x17cm-Format benutzt. Spierings Panoramafotos wurden in mehreren Ausstellungen im Bodenseeraum gezeigt und liegen in mehreren Fotobänden vor, darunter „Bodensee" (2006) und „Schwarzwald" (2008) in der Edition Panorama Bibliothek. Ausgedehnte Streifzüge zu allen Tages- und Jahreszeiten im gesamten Bodenseegebiet lassen sein Bildarchiv beständig wachsen. *Since 1999, Holger Spiering has devoted himself particularly to panoramic photography, for which he uses two Fuji medium-format cameras with the unusual 6x17 cm format. Spiering's panoramic photos have been displayed at several exhibitions in the Lake Constance region, and have also appeared in several illustrated volumes, including "Bodensee" (2006) and "Schwarzwald" (2008) in the Edition Panorama Bibliothek. With extended forays at all times of the day and year throughout the Lake Constance region, his picture archive is growing steadily.* www.bodenseefotografie.de.

IRIS LEMANCZYK

Iris Lemanczyk wurde 1964 in Kirchheim/Teck bei Stuttgart geboren. Schon während des Germanistik- und Geographie Studiums in Tübingen lockte immer wieder die Ferne. Gleich nach ihrem Studienabschluss packte sie den Rucksack und reiste mit einer Freundin für Monate um die Welt. *Iris Lemanczyk was born in 1964 in Kirchheim/Teck near Stuttgart. Even while studying German and geography in Tübingen, she was attracted by the lure of far-distant places. As soon as she completed her studies, she packed her rucksack, and together with a friend travelled for months around the world.*

Wieder zurück in Süddeutschland volontierte und arbeitete sie als Zeitungs-Redakteurin bei der „Neuen Württembergischen Zeitung" in Göppingen und bei der „Südwest Presse" in Ulm. Zwischendurch ging Iris Lemanczyk für einige Zeit nach Namibia, arbeitete dort bei der deutschsprachigen „Allgemeinen Zeitung" als Sportredakteurin. Dafür musste sie die komplizierten Regeln von Sportarten wie Cricket und Bowls lernen. Und sie musste sich in Gelassenheit üben, wenn manchmal das für sie exotische Getier über die Schreibtische der Windhoeker Redaktionsstube krabbelte. *Back again in southern Germany, she volunteered and worked as a newspaper editor for the "Neue Württembergische Zeitung" in Göppingen and at the "Südwest Presse" in Ulm. In between, Iris Lemanczyk spent some time in Namibia, where she worked for the German-language "Allgemeine Zeitung" as a sports editor, having to learn the complicated rules of such sports as cricket and bowls. And she had to practice her composure when the exotic insects of the region were sometimes found crawling over the desks of the Windhoek editorial office.*

Seit 1997 ist Iris Lemanczyk freiberuflich tätig. Sie schreibt Kinder- und Jugendbücher sowie Sachbücher, verfasst Reiseberichte und ist als Dozentin für Kreatives Schreiben tätig. Wann immer es möglich oder auch beruflich erforderlich ist, begibt sie sich auf Reisen. So besuchte sie einige Monate Australien und Neuseeland, recherchierte in Indien, Tibet, aber auch in Kambodscha, Kenia und Madagaskar. *Since 1997, Iris Lemanczyk has worked as a freelancer, writing children's books and non-fiction and compiling travel reports, and also works as a lecturer on creative writing. Whenever possible, or necessary for her work, she sets off again on her travels. She has spent several months in Australia and New Zealand, researched in India and Tibet, and also in Cambodia, Kenya and Madagascar.*

Doch es ist nicht nur die Ferne, die sie fasziniert. Schwäbische Alb, Schwarzwald, Bayern und Bodensee, die bei der Stuttgarterin vor der Haustür liegen, kennt sie durch viele Wanderungen, zu Fuß oder mit Langlaufskiern, sommers wie winters. *But she is fascinated not only by far-off places. From her many tours on foot or cross-country skis, in summer or winter, she also knows the Schwäbische Alb, the Black Forest, Bavaria and the Lake Constance which lie close to her Stuttgart home.* www.irislemanczyk.de

Leiblach

Bregenzer Ach

Österreich

Bregenz

Dornbirner Ach

Hard

Lindau

Nonnenhorn

Kressbronn

Wasserburg

Langenargen

Rhein

Alter Rhein

Rheintaler Bhmenkanal

Altenhein

Schussen

Friedrichshafen

OBERSEE

Rorschach

Horn

Rotach

Deutschland

Immenstaad

Arbon

Steinach

Goldach

Hagnau

Romanshorn

Aach

Willerbach

Seefelder Aach

Meersburg

St. Gallen

Unteruhldingen

Birnau

Altnau

Überlingen

Konstanz

Mainau

Kreuzlingen

ÜBERLINGER SEE

Dingelsdorf

Wallhausen

Litzelstetten

Gottlieben

SCHWEIZER SEERÜCKEN

Sipplingen

Allensbach

Triboltingen

BODANRÜCK

Reichenau

Ermatingen

Ludwigshafen

Mannenbach

Mndelsee

Berlingen

Steckborn

Schweiz

UNTERSEE

Bodman

Radolfzell

Horn

Izang

HÖRI

Gaienhofen

Stockacher Aach

Moos

Hemmenhofen

Wangen

Mammern

Stein am Rhein

Öhningen

Radolfzeller Aach

Rhein

Schaffhausen

BODENSEE

IM WANDEL DER ZEIT *LAKE CONSTANCE – IN CHANGING TIMES*

Das Wasser glitzert, weiße Segel schmücken den See, Schiff wiegt sich in der leichten Brise, dahinter verschwimmen die Schweizer Alpen mit ihren schneebedeckten Gipfeln im Dunst: Bodensee-Idyll im Sommer. Nebel, der die Sicht trübt, das Gemüt drückt und die Orientierung erschwert. Bodenseestimmung im Herbst. *The water glitters, white sails dot the lake, reeds wave in the gentle breeze, the Swiss Alps with their snow-covered peaks in the background are blurred in the haze: the idyll of Lake Constance in the summer. Mist which clouds the sight, mutes the splashing of the waves, weighs on the mind and makes orientation difficult. Lake Constance in an autumn mood.*

„Wenn Junitage durch die Blätterkronen brausen und die Wasseroberfläche in Gefunkel zerspringt, tut der See mittelmeerisch. Von Spätherbst bis Vorfrühling führen ihn Stürme weißgrün vor, da spielt er Fjord. Dieser See spielt alles nur. Identität gedeiht hier schwach. Das Klimatheater, das auf der anpassungssüchtigen Seebühne seine pausenlose Unbeständigkeits- und Überraschungsdramaturgie betreibt, will, dass wir uns an nichts halten als an den Wechsel", schrieb der Schriftsteller und Bodenseeanwohner Martin Walser 1978 in „Heimatlob", einer Art Liebeserklärung an den Bodensee. *"When June days hum through the treetops and the surface of the water bursts into a sparkling mosaic, the lake looks Mediterranean. From late autumn to early spring, storms turn it white-green; then it plays the fjord. This lake plays everything. Identity thrives only weakly here. The climatic play, which presents its unending drama of volatility and surprise on the ever-changing stage of the lake, wants us to be able to hold onto nothing more than the fact of change itself", wrote the author and Lake Constance resident Martin Walser in 1978 in "Heimatlob", a sort of declaration of love to Lake Constance.*

Der See mit seinen vielen Gesichtern. Der Wechsel. Wechselvoll auch seine Namen: „Lacus Lemannus", „Lacus Constantinus", „Konstanzer See, „Lacus Brigantium", „Bregenzer See, und „Lacus Bodamicus" – Bodamicus, das Dorf Bodman, dort, wo einst eine karolingische Königspfalz stand. Bodman, das Dorf „auf dem Boden", im Gegensatz zu den Siedlungen, die am Hochufer lagen. Walahfrid Strabo, der bedeutende Abt der Insel Reichenau, nannte den Bodensee „Potamicus". Er bevorzugte diesen Namen, vom griechischen Wort für Fluss, Potamos, abgeleitet, anstatt von der weltlichen Königspfalz Bodman. Doch für die Menschen am See, in der Dichtung, im Volksmund und beim Handel, hielt sich der Name „Bodamicus" hartnäckig. Aus „Bodamicus" wurde Bodensee. *The lake with its many faces. The change. Its name is just as changeable: "Lacus Lemannus", "Lake Alamannen, "Lacus Constantinus", Lake Constance, "Lacus Brigantium", "Lake Bregenz, and "Lacus Bodamicus" – Bodamicus, the village of Bodman, the site of a former Carolingian royal palatinate. Bodman, the village "on the ground", in contrast to the settlements higher up on the banks. Walahfrid Strabo, the eminent Abbot of the island of Reichenau, called Lake Constance "Potamicus". He preferred this name, which is derived from the Greek word for river – Potamos – instead of from the secular royal palatinate Bodman. But for the people on the lake, in literature, in common parlance and in trade, the name "Bodamicus" persisted stubbornly. "Bodamicus" became "Bodensee".*

Der Bodensee ist entstanden durch den mächtigen Rheingletscher. In der Riss-Eiszeit vor 200.000 Jahren war vom See noch nichts zu sehen. Der Rheingletscher schob sich von den Alpen bis über die Donau hinaus. Die Eiswüste erstickte über 100.000 Jahre lang jedes Leben unter ihrem viele hundert Meter dicken Eispanzer. Danach kamen Wärmeperioden, in denen die Natur die vom Eis befreite Landschaft zurückeroberte. Ein tiefer See, vom Schmelzwasser des Rheins gespeist, blieb zurück. Enten, Pelikane und Seeadler lebten in seinen Schilfflächen. Tausende von Tümpeln und Seen entstanden. Doch das Idyll währte nicht lange. In der Würm-Eiszeit vor 30.000 Jahren schob sich der Rheingletscher abermals über den Bodensee. Nach dem Abschmelzen des Eises, vor etwa 10.000 Jahren, nahm der Bodensee eine Fläche von etwa 1200 Quadratkilometern ein, war also mehr als doppelt so groß wie heute. Erdgeschichtlich betrachtet ist der See nur eine temporäre Erscheinung, die es in einigen zehntausend Jahren nicht mehr geben wird. Er verlandet. Heute jedoch ist er mit seinen 534 Quadratkilometern Wasseroberfläche und seinen 273 Kilometern Ufer eines der größten Binnengewässer Europas. *Lake Constance was created by the huge Rhein glacier. In the Riss Ice Age 200,000 years ago, there was nothing yet to be seen of the lake. The Rhein glacier thrust its way from the Alps to the Danube and beyond. For over 100,000 years, this wilderness of ice smothered all life beneath its armour several hundred meters thick. This was followed by warm periods, during which nature reconquered the landscape now freed of ice. A deep lake remained, fed by the meltwater of the Rhein. Ducks, pelicans and sea eagles lived in its reed beds. Thousands of ponds and lakes were created. But this idyll did not endure for long. In the Würm Ice Age 30,000 years ago, the Rhein glacier once again spread its icy grip over Lake Constance. After the ice melted about 10,000 years ago, Lake Constance covered an area of about 1,200 km², more than twice its present area. In terms of the history of the earth, the lake is nothing but a temporary phenomenon, which will not exist in a few tens of thousands of years. It is returning to the land. Today however, with its 534 km² of water surface and 273 kilometres of shoreline, it is one of the largest stretches of inland water in Europe.*

Der Bodensee liegt im Dreiländereck Deutschland, Österreich, Schweiz, wobei Deutschland mit 173 Uferkilometern den größten Anteil hat. Wem exakt welcher Teil des Gewässers gehört, wurde nie festgelegt, die Grenzziehungen durch den See beruhen allein auf Gewohnheitsrecht. Namentlich gliedert sich der Bodensee in drei Teile: Das größte Stück (472 Quadratkilometer) zwischen Lindau und Meersburg heißt Obersee. Der Überlinger See erstreckt sich zwischen Meersburg und Bodman. Untersee nennt man den Teil zwischen Konstanz und Stein am Rhein. Der Untersee gliedert sich in den Gnadensee, der im Norden vor Allensbach liegt, und den Zeller See im Süden zwischen Horn und Radolfzell. Elf Inseln gibt es, die drei größten davon sind: Reichenau, Mainau und Lindau. *Lake Constance lies at the junction of three countries, Germany, Austria and Switzerland, with Germany having the largest share of the shoreline at 173 kilometres. Who owns exactly which part of the lake has never been established, and the borderlines through the lake are based solely on common law and accepted practice. Lake Constance can be divided into three sections: the largest section (472 km²) between Lindau and Meersburg is called the "Obersee". The "Überlinger See" extends between Meersburg and Bodman. The "Untersee" is the name given to the section between Konstanz and Stein am Rhein. The Untersee is divided into the "Gnadensee" in the north before Allensbach and the "Zeller See" in the south between Horn and Radolfzell. There are eleven islands, of which the largest are Reichenau, Mainau and Lindau.*

Schon Jahrtausende vor den Römern, Mönchen und Ausflugsbooten war das Ufer besiedelt. In der Jungsteinzeit, um 4400 vor unserer Zeitrechnung, rammten erste Siedler Pfähle in den weichen Uferschlick. Als deren Überreste im 19. Jahrhundert wieder zutage traten, dachten ihre Entdecker, die Steinzeitmenschen hätten ganze Dörfer auf Pfählen in den See gestellt. Archäologen korrigierten, sie gingen davon aus, dass die Hütten nicht im See, sondern am Ufer standen. Auf Stelzen stellte man die Häuser, um die Schwankungen des Wasserspiegels von bis zu zwei Metern ohne nasses Hab und Gut zu überstehen. *The lakeshore was settled thousands of years ago, long before the Romans, monks and excursion boats arrived. In the Neolithic period, around 4,400 BC, the first settlers rammed piles into the soft mud of the bank. When their remains came to light again in the 19th Century, it was first thought by their discoverers that the Stone Age people built whole villages on piles in the lake. Archaeologists corrected them, considering that the huts stood not in the lake, but on the banks. The houses were set on piles in order to survive the fluctuations in the water level of up to 2 m without having all their goods and chattels soaked.*

In jüngster Zeit fanden Archäologen heraus, dass wahrscheinlich vereinzelte Pfahlbauten doch im See standen. Durch die Lage am Alpenrand war die Region schon früh Durchzugsgebiet und Handelsraum. Die Kelten errichteten befestigte Siedlungen. Im Auftrag des Kaisers Augustus erschienen die Römer im Jahr 15. Rund um den See errichteten sie Kastelle, um Kelten und Räter unter Kontrolle zu halten. *In more recent times, archaeologists found out that there were probably isolated pile constructions actually in the lake. Due to its location on the edge of the Alps, the region was from early times a transit point and trading area. The Celts constructed fortified settlements. On the orders of Emperor Augustus, the Romans appeared in the year 15, and built forts all around the lake in order to keep the Celts and Raeti under control.*

„Die Einsamkeit hier ist rau und voller Wasser. Sie hat hohe Berge und enge Täler, dazu vielerlei Tiere, Bären, Rudel von Wölfen und Wildschweinen. Ich fürchte, sie fallen über dich her, wenn ich dich dorthin bringe." Äußerst besorgt schrieb im Jahre 612 der Diakon Hiltibold aus Arbon dem Mönch Gallus, der aus Irland gekommen war und den Plan hatte, mitten im wilden Hinterland des Sees ein Bethaus zu bauen. Beseelt von dem Gedanken, das Lob Gottes in die Welt zu tragen, war Gallus aber keine Anstrengung zu groß. Er wollte missionieren. Dieser Eifer war Triebfeder, um den Bodenseeraum zu kultivieren. *"The solitude here is rough and full of water. There are high mountains and narrow valleys, as well as many animals, bears, packs of wolves and wild pigs. I fear they will attack you if I bring you there." So wrote Deacon Hiltibold from Arbon very worriedly in the year 612 to the monk Gallus, who had come from Ireland and planned to build a prayer house in the wild hinterland of the lake. Inspired by the idea of bringing the praise of God to the world, no effort was too great for Gallus. He wanted to proselytise. This zeal was the driving force behind the cultivation of the Lake Constance area.*

Die Klöster prägten das Gebiet, allen voran jene in St. Gallen und auf der Reichenau, aber auch die in Stein am Rhein, Konstanz, Kreuzlingen, Bregenz und Salem. Die Ordensleute ließen Kirchen mit herrlichen Fresken bauen, die vom Christentum erzählen. Lindau, Überlingen und Konstanz verdanken ihren mittelalterlichen Reichtum ihrer Bedeutung als Verkehrsknotenpunkte und Handelsplätze. Der See wurde verbindendes Element über Ländergrenzen hinweg. *The area came to be characterised by monasteries, above all those in St. Gallen and on Reichenau, but also those in Stein am Rhein, Konstanz, Kreuzlingen, Bregenz and Salem. The clerics had churches built, with wonderful frescoes depicting the story of Christendom. Art and culture developed as the lake became an increasingly popular transport hub. Lindau, Überlingen and Konstanz owed their mediaeval wealth to their importance as traffic hubs and trading centres. The lake became the connecting element across national boundaries.*

Und er war schon immer wichtigster Klimafaktor. Die Wasserfläche wirkt als riesiger Spiegel, der das Sonnenlicht reflektiert und in einer Zone von vier bis fünf Kilometer über das Ufer hinaus die Sonnenintensität zusätzlich steigert. Die Wassermassen speichern die Wärme und mäßigen sowohl Winter als auch Sommer. Dadurch entspricht das Klima etwa dem der Oberrheinebene, die 200 bis 300 Meter tiefer liegt. Der Föhn strömt häufig durch das Rheintal zum See, bringt warme Luft und klare Sicht. Im Winter allerdings hängt oft eine hartnäckige, aufs Gemüt drückende Hochnebeldecke über dem See. *And it has always been the most important climatic factor. The water surface acts like a giant mirror, which reflects the sunlight, and within an area of four to five kilometres beyond the shore further increases the intensity of the sunshine. The masses of water store the heat, making both winter and summer more temperate. The climate is therefore similar to that of the Upper Rhein plain, which is nearly 1,000 ft. lower down. The "Föhn" frequently flows through the Rhein valley to the lake, bringing warm air and good visibility. In winter however, the lake is often shrouded in a thick, stubborn blanket of mist, which depresses the spirit.*

Das milde Klima und der gute Boden haben seit jeher die Landwirtschaft begünstigt. Kein Wunder also, dass sich die Reichenauer Benediktinermönche schon früh mit dem Gartenbau beschäftigten. Der Abt Walahfrid Strabo schrieb Anfang des 9. Jahrhunderts „Liber de cultura hortorum", das erste Lehrbuch über den Gartenbau. Die Römer kannten bereits acht Apfel- und 17 Birnensorten, doch die Mönche wollten noch mehr. In den Klostergärten experimentierten sie mit neuen Obst- und Gemüsesorten und weiteten die landwirtschaftliche Nutzung aus. *The mild climate and the fertile soil have always favoured agriculture. No wonder therefore that the Benedictine monks of Reichenau soon became involved in market gardening. At the beginning of the 9th Century, Abbot Walahfrid Strabo wrote his "Liber de cultura hortorum", the first textbook on market gardening. The Romans already knew eight varieties of apples and 17 varieties of pears, but the monks wanted more. In the monastery gardens, they experimented with new varieties of fruit and vegetables and extended the agricultural land usage.*

„Alles ist in reichem Überfluss vorhanden, was notwendig, nützlich oder angenehm ist für Menschen und Tiere, und alles was man sich nur wünschen kann", schrieb Benedikt de Pileo aus Italien, der am Konstanzer Konzil teilnahm, das von 1414 bis 1418 dauerte. In Konstanz, das selbst kaum 6.000 Einwohner zählte, wurden damals 60.000 Gäste bewirtet. *"Everything which is necessary, useful or pleasant for people and animals, and everything one could wish for, is available here in rich abundance", wrote Benedikt de Pileo from Italy, who attended the Council of Constance, which lasted from 1414 to 1418. In Constance, which itself numbered hardly 6,000 inhabitants, 60,000 guests were accommodated at the time.*

Sowohl im schweizerischen Thurgau als auch in Deutschland sind die meisten Streuobstwiesen im 20. Jahrhundert durch Plantagen ersetzt worden. Heute erstreckt sich am Bodensee das größte deutsche Anbaugebiet für Kernobst. Jeder fünfte Apfel, der in Deutschland reift, hängt am Bodensee am Baum. Allein 220.000 Tonnen Äpfel werden pro Jahr geerntet. Wenn nicht ein Großteil der Ernte durch Unwetter beschädigt wird. Hagelnetze, die die Obstplantagen überdecken, sollen das Obst schützen. Denn einmal vom Hagelkorn getroffen wird ein Tafelapfel sofort zum Mostobst degradiert. *Both in Swiss Thurgau and in Germany, most fruit meadows were replaced in the 20th Century by plantations. Today, the largest German cultivation centre for stone fruit can be found around the shores of Lake Constance. 20% of the apples grown in Germany come from the trees around Lake Constance. 220,000 tonnes of apples alone are harvested annually. Provided that a large part of the harvest is not damaged by bad weather. The fruit plantations are covered by nets to protect them against hail, because if once hit by hailstones, an eating apple is immediately downgraded for use in processing.*

Die einschneidendste Veränderung der Bodenseelandschaft begann mit der Industrialisierung. Erste Textilfabriken entstanden am See, die die Wasserkraft der Flüsse Schussen und Riss nutzten. Die Eisenbahn kam 1850 bis Friedrichshafen, 1854 bis Lindau, Raddampfer ersetzten Lastensegler. Der Handel nahm zu, der Fremdenverkehr entwickelte sich.

The most drastic change to the Lake Constance landscape began with industrialisation. The first textile factories were built around the lake, using the water power of the rivers Schussen and Riss. The railway system was extended to Friedrichshafen by 1850, and at Güttingen, the cycle path around the lake, the Rhein Falls at Schaffhausen, a sailing trip, the impenetrable silence of a misty morning or simply the glittering of the lake in the light of the setting sun.

Touristisch ist der Bodensee heute zweigeteilt. Während auf der deutschen Uferseite von ihm als „Riviera" gesprochen wird und Städte wie Lindau, Meersburg oder Konstanz zu den beliebtesten Reisezielen in Süddeutschland gehören und auch die Österreicher, dank der Bregenzer Festspiele, touristisch gut dastehen, scheint die Schweizer Seite eher touristische Provinz zu sein. Vom Massentourismus bleiben vor allem die Thurgauer verschont.

In terms of tourism, Lake Constance consists of two parts. While the German shore is referred to as a "Riviera", and towns such as Lindau, Meersburg and Konstanz are amongst the most popular holiday destinations in southern Germany, and the Austrians are also well off for tourists thanks to the Bregenz Festival Plays, the Swiss side is rather provincial when it comes to tourism. Thurgau in particular has been spared mass tourism.

Die Grenzen des Wachstums waren in den siebziger Jahren erreicht. Der Bodenseekreis wies das dichteste Straßennetz aller deutschen Landkreise auf. Und nur 30 der 160 Kilometer des baden-württembergischen Bodenseeufers besaßen noch einen einigermaßen natürlichen Charakter. Die Einleitung von Abwässern und ausgeschwemmten Düngemitteln ließ den See beinahe kippen.

The limits of growth were reached in the 1970s. The Lake Constance district had the densest road network of any German district. And only 30 of the 160 kilometres of the Baden-Württemberg shore of Lake Constance still retained anything of their natural character. The introduction of waste water, and fertilisers washed out of the surrounding land, almost destroyed the ecological balance of the lake.

Es musste dringend gehandelt werden. Kläranlagen wurden gebaut und Naturschutzgebiete ausgewiesen, denn das Wollmatinger Ried sollte zugunsten von Baugebieten verkleinert werden, und der Halbinsel Mettnau mitsamt der Süddeutschen Vogelwarte drohte der Bau eines riesigen Freizeitzentrums. Heute sind am Untersee und am Überlinger See die naturbelassenen Ufer als „Naturschutzgebiet Bodensee" ausgewiesen. Der Gedanke, dass eine intakte Erholungslandschaft ein wirtschaftliches Kapital ist, hat sich am Bodensee mittlerweile längst verfestigt.

Urgent action had to be taken. Water treatment plants were constructed and nature preservation areas established, because the "Wollmatinger Ried" was to be reduced in size to provide building land, and the Mettnau peninsula together with the "Süddeutsche Vogelwarte" ("South-German ornithological station") were threatened by the construction of an enormous leisure centre. Today, the unspoilt natural shores of the Untersee and Überlinger See have been designated the "Lake Constance Nature Preservation Area". The idea that an intact recreational landscape represents economic capital has long since been accepted at Lake Constance.

„Der See ist ein Freund", schreibt Walser in „Heimatlob". So bleibt der Bodensee einzigartig wie ein Freund. Jeder mag etwas anderes an ihm; sei es nun der Badestrand am Malereck, das Kornhaus von Rorschach, ein Aussichtspunkt auf dem Seerücken bei Güttingen, der Radweg rund um den See, die Höri mit ihrer Vergangenheit als Künstlerkolonie, der Rheinfall bei Schaffhausen, ein Segeltörn, die undurchsichtige Geräuschlosigkeit eines Nebelmorgens oder einfach nur das Glitzern des Sees im Abendlicht.

"The lake is a friend", writes Walser in "Heimatlob". And Lake Constance remains as unique and individual as a friend. Everyone likes something different about it: whether this is the bathing beach at the Malereck (painters' corner), the "Kornhaus" at Rorschach, an observation point on the "Seerücken" at Güttingen, the cycle path around the lake, the Rhein Falls at Schaffhausen, a sailing trip, the impenetrable silence of a misty morning or simply the glittering of the lake in the light of the setting sun.

„DIE TRINKEN UNS DEN SEE LEER"
"They're Drinking Our Lake Dry"

„Die trinken uns den See leer", befürchteten Anrainer, als 1958 der „Zweckverband Bodenseewasserversorgung" gegründet wurde. Heute werden nicht mehr als vier Millionen Menschen zwischen Überlingen und Stuttgart mit Bodenseewasser versorgt, aber leer getrunken haben sie ihn immer noch nicht. Jährlich fließen nämlich mehr als elf Milliarden Kubikmeter Wasser aus dem Rhein und den übrigen Zuflüssen in den Bodensee, davon zapft die Wasserversorgung gerade mal 130 Millionen Kubikmeter ab. Damit ist der Bodensee der größte Trinkwasserspeicher Europas.

"They're drinking our lake dry", local residents feared, when the "Zweckverband Bodenseewasserversorgung" ("Lake Constance water supply association") was founded in 1958. Today, more than 4 million people living between Überlingen and Stuttgart are supplied with water from Lake Constance, but they still have not drunk it dry. Every year, more than 11 billion m³ of water flow from the Rhein and other tributaries into Lake Constance, of which the water supply draws off only around 130 million m³, making Lake Constance the largest freshwater reservoir in Europe.

Während Segler, Surfer und Badende sich an der Wasseroberfläche vergnügen, bewahren die Tiefen des Sees einen ungeheuren Schatz: sauberes Wasser von Trinkwasserqualität. In Sipplingen pumpt man aus 60 Meter Tiefe klares, sauberes Wasser aus dem See. Trotzdem durchläuft das Bodenseewasser noch drei Reinigungsstufen, bis es als Trinkwasser höchster Güte durch ein 1.700 Kilometer umfassendes Fernleitungsnetz mit mehr als zwei Meter dicken Rohren in die Haushalte fließt. Selbst in den heißesten Sommern wird der Bodensee nicht geleert.

While sailors, surfers and bathers enjoy themselves on the surface, the depths of the lake harbour a vast treasure: clean water of potable quality. In Sipplingen, clear, clean water is pumped out of the lake from a depth of 200ft. The Lake Constance water still goes through three treatment stages before being supplied to households as drinking water of the highest quality through a 1,700 kilometre long-distance piping system with pipes more than 2 m in diameter. Even in the hottest summers, Lake Constance is not drained.

Dem Schutz der Trinkwasserreserven unserer Erde hat sich die Umweltinitiative „Living Lakes" verschrieben. Vom Titicaca-See in Bolivien und Peru zum mexikanischen Chapala See, vom russischen Baikalsee, dem japanischen Biwa See oder dem afrikanischen Viktoria See bis zum ungarischen Plattensee und natürlich dem Bodensee gehören 58 Seen auf fünf Kontinenten zu „Living Lakes", dem Seen-Netzwerk. Die Initiative möchte weltweit auf die Probleme in und an den Seen und damit der Trinkwasserreserven aufmerksam machen.

The environmental initiative "Living Lakes" has committed itself to the protection of the fresh water reserves of our planet. From Lake Titicaca in Bolivia and Peru to the Mexican Lake Chapala, from the Russian Lake Baikal, the Japanese Lake Biwa or the African Lake Victoria to the

UND IMMER WIEDER FELCHEN *WHITEFISH AND MORE WHITEFISH*

Zander und Hecht räubern vorwiegend in der flacheren Uferzone. Felchen, Seeforellen und Saiblinge zieht es hinaus in den See. 35 Fischarten leben im Bodensee. Von Fischen haben sich bereits die Pfahl-bau-Siedler ernährt. Wenn sie auch mit Fischen gehandelt haben, ist es vermutlich das älteste Gewerbe

am See. Heute leben noch etwa 150 Berufsfischer vom Fischfang, hinzu kommen Tausende von Hobby-anglern. Obwohl der Bodensee den Fischen einen gewaltigen Lebensraum bietet, nehmen die Fang-quoten seit den siebziger Jahren ständig ab. Die strenge Reglementierung der Fangmengen hat genau-so wenig Schuld wie die fischfressenden Kormorane, die mancher Fischer am Untersee zu seinen Feinden erklärt hat. Vielmehr ist es das saubere Wasser, das zu einer Abnahme der Fischpopulation geführt hat. Ist das Wasser sauber, existieren wenig Algen. Wo wenig Algen sind, gibt es auch wenig Wasserflöhe, die den Fischen als Nahrung dienen. Haben die Fische weniger zu fressen, vermehren sie sich nicht so stark. *Zander and pike hunt mainly in the flatter areas of the shore, while whitefish, sea trout and char live further out in the lake. 35 species of fish live in Lake Constance. The pile-builders of 6,000 years ago ate fish caught in the lake. If they also traded in fish, this was probably the oldest trade conducted on the lake. Today there are still around 150 commercial fishermen who live off the lake, to-*

gether with thousands of leisure anglers. Although Lake Constance offers the fish a tremendous habitat, the fishing quotas have declined steadily since the 1970s. The strict regulation of catches is therefore just as little to blame as the fish-eating cormorants, which many fishermen on the Untersee regard as com-petitors and enemies. It is much rather the clean water which has led to the decline in the fish population. If the water is clean, it contains fewer algae. Where there are few algae, there is also little daphnia for the fish to feed on. And when the fish have less to eat, they breed in fewer numbers.

Von 800 bis 1,300 Tonnen Fisch, die jährlich am Bodensee gefangen werden, sind mehr als die Hälfte Felchen. Er gehört zu den Salmoniden, zur gleichen Familie wie Lachs und Forelle. Der Appetit auf

Felchen ist am Bodensee so groß, dass Nachschub aus dem Ausland, hauptsächlich aus Ungarn, zuge-kauft wird. *Of the 800 to 1,300 tonnes of fish caught every year in Lake Constance, more than half is whitefish. This is one of the salmonides, belonging to the same family as salmon and trout. The appetite for whitefish on Lake Constance is so great that extra supplies have to be bought in from abroad, mainly from Hungary.*

Egli oder Kretzer, wie die kleine Barschsorte nur hier genannt wird, steht an zweiter Stelle in der Fang-liste. Seltener sind Aal, Seeforelle, Hecht, Zander und Saibling, die die Fischer im Morgengrauen aus ihren Netzen holen. *"Egli" or "Kretzer", as the small species of perch is called here, comes second on the catch list. Less common are eel, sea trout, pike, zander and char, which the fishermen collect from their nets in the early morning light.*

Die Römer haben den Weinbau an den Bodensee gebracht. Seine Blütezeit hatte er jedoch im Mittelalter, als sich zwischen Friedrichshafen und Überlingen eine geschlossene Reblandschaft erstreckte, die dem Kloster Salem gehörte. Doch aus den alten Sorten wie dem „Elbling" ließ sich nur ein saurer Trunk keltern. Wahrlich kein Renner in den Klöstern, zumal die Kirchenmänner oft über gute Kontakte nach Italien verfügten und sich von dort bessere Weine kommen ließen. Da Wasser aber häufig mit Krankheitskeimen belastet war, galt Wein als gesundes Getränk. Soldaten und Arbeiter hatten Anrecht auf bis zu drei Liter Wein pro Tag, sodass bei der Weinproduktion Quantität und nicht unbedingt die Qualität im Vordergrund stand. *It was the Romans who brought wine-growing to Lake Constance, although it was not until the Middle Ages that it experienced its heyday, when a vineyard landscape belonging to the monastery of Salem stretched between Friedrichshafen and Überlingen. However, only an acidic drink could be pressed from the old varieties of vine such as the "Elbling". Certainly not a great hit in the monasteries, especially since the clerics often had good contacts with Italy, from where they obtained better wines. Since water at the time was frequently contaminated with germs, wine was considered to be a healthy drink. Soldiers and labourers were entitled to up to three litres of wine per day, so that wine production focused on quantity, and not necessarily on quality.*

Doch die Lage am See, der das Sonnenlicht nicht nur reflektiert, sondern auch die Wärme speichert, bekommt den Reben gut. Außerdem werden die Temperaturen durch den See gemildert, sodass es im Winter weniger Frosttage gibt. Als im 18. Jahrhundert neue Sorten nach neuen Methoden angebaut wurden, wandelte sich auch die Qualität. *But the location on the lake, which not only reflects the sunlight but also stores the heat, is good for the vines. The temperatures are also moderated by the lake, so that there are fewer frosty days in winter. When new varieties started to be cultivated using new methods in the 18th Century, the quality was also transformed.*

Liebling unter den Bodensee-Weißweinen ist heute der Müller-Thurgau, der 1882 von Hermann Müller-Thurgau am Untersee entwickelt wurde. Und der Meersburger Weißherbst, ein besonders aromatischer Rosé. Die Soldaten und Arbeiter, aber auch die Kirchenmänner von anno dazumal würden wahrscheinlich bei der Qualität der heutigen Weine ihren Gaumen nicht trauen. Oder begeistert schmatzen und nach mehr verlangen. *The favourite amongst the Lake Constance white wines is today the Müller-Thurgau, which was developed in 1882 by Hermann Müller from Tägerwilen in Thurgau on the Untersee. And the "Meersburger Weißherbst", a particularly aromatic rosé. The soldiers and labourers, and also the churchmen of those earlier times would probably not believe their lips in appreciation and ask for more.*

AUSNAHMEZUSTAND: SEEGFRÖRNE *MERRY HELL: "SEEGFRÖRNE"*

Aus Eis ist der Bodensee entstanden. Eis ist auch heute noch eine Besonderheit am See, dann, wenn die Wasseroberfläche zur begehbaren Eisdecke gefriert. Recht häufig geschieht das im Gnadensee zwischen Allensbach und der Insel Reichenau, noch häufiger vor dem Wollmatinger Ried zwischen Hegne und der Reichenau. Dann werden die Schlittschuhe ausgepackt, und Eisfischer, die am See „Zocker" genannt werden, schlagen tellergroße Löcher ins Eis und üben sich in Geduld. *Lake Constance was created from ice. It is today still a very special time on the lake when the water surface freezes to a covering of ice thick enough to walk on. This happens very frequently on the Gnadensee between Allensbach and the island of Reichenau, and even more frequently before the Wollmatinger Ried between Hegne and Reichenau. Then the ice skates are unpacked, and ice fishermen, known on the lake as "Zocker", knock plate-sized holes in the ice and patiently wait for a bite.*

Viel seltener passiert es, dass der gesamte See zufriert, so wie am 6. Februar 1963. Zum ersten Mal seit 133 Jahren konnte der See wieder begangen werden. Bei dieser „Seegfröne", wie das Überfrieren des Sees von den Einheimischen genannt wird, herrschte Ausnahmezustand: Pferde traben auf dem Eis, Autos fahren über den See, Flugzeuge landen bei ihren Eisflügen auf der Eisschicht, und zwischen Lindau und Konstanz werden Briefe mit Sonderstempel per „Eisluftpost" befördert. Sogar der Gemeinderat tagt auf dem Eis. *It is much rarer for the whole lake to freeze over, as it did on 6th February 1963. For the first time in 133 years, the lake could be walked on again. When this "Seegfröne" happens, as the freezing over of the lake is called by the local population, merry hell breaks loose: horses trot over the ice, cars drive over the lake, aircraft land on the ice sheets on their "ice flights", and between Lindau and Konstanz, letters are delivered carrying the special stamp by "Eisluftpost" ("ice air mail"). Even the local council holds its meetings on the ice.*

Am 12. Februar hielten die „Seegfröne" immer noch an und die Münsterlinger und Hagnauer eine gemeinsame Tradition von 1573 aufrecht: Die Büste des Evangelisten Johannes soll bei einer „Seegfröne" in einer Prozession in die jeweilige am anderen Ufer liegende Kirche getragen werden. Natürlich über das Eis. Während sich die Hagnauer im Februar 1830 nach Münsterlingen aufmachten, um nach dem Genuss einer warmen Suppe im Kloster das Bild des Johannes zurück in die Hagnauer Pfarrkirche zu holen, kamen die Münsterlinger 1963 mit drei Fässern Wein auf ihren Schlitten und mehr als 2.500 Teilnehmern nach Hagnau. Sie brachten die Büste wieder in die Münsterlinger Klosterkirche. Dort harrt sie der nächsten Kältewelle. *By the 12th February, the "Seegfröne" still persisted, and the people of Münsterlingen and Hagnau observed a joint tradition going back to 1573: whenever a "Seegfröne" happens, the bust of John the Evangelist is carried in procession to the church on the opposite shore. Over the ice, of course. While the people of Hagnau set off for Münsterlingen in February 1830, to enjoy a bowl of warm soup in the monastery before carrying the bust back to the Hagnau Parish Church, the people of Münsterlingen arrived in Hagnau in 1963 with three barrels of wine on their sledges, and a procession of over 2500 people. They carried the bust back to the Münsterlingen Parish Church, where it remains until the next wave of extremely cold weather.*

Dann begann das große Tauen. Am 10. März fuhren die Fähren zwischen Konstanz und Meersburg wieder. *Then began the great thaw. By 10th March, the ferries were running again between Konstanz and Meersburg.*

Auch in Gustav Schwabs Gedicht „Der Reiter und der Bodensee" gehts um eine „Seegfröne". Ein Reiter überquert ahnungslos den zugefrorenen See. Als man ihm sagt, welche Strecke er gerade glücklich überwunden hat, bricht er – vom Schreck getroffen – tot zusammen. *Gustav Schwab's poem "Der Reiter und der Bodensee" also features a "Seegfröne". A rider crosses the frozen lake without realising what he is doing. When he is told what he has just done, he immediately drops down dead from fear.*

Den Schriftsteller Peter Handke inspirierte das Gedicht zu seinem Schauspiel „Der Ritt über den Bodensee".

This was the poem which inspired the playwright Peter Handke to pen his play "Der Ritt über den Bodensee".

Die wievielte „Seegfröne" die von 1963 gewesen ist, ist ungewiss. Manche Veröffentlichungen verzeichnen 33, manche 34 seit dem Jahr 875. Unsicher ist auch, wann und ob es überhaupt eine neue „Seegfröne" geben wird, denn am See wird es wärmer. *What number "Seegfröne" the one of 1963 actually was is uncertain. Some publications record it as the 33rd, some the 34th since the year 875. It is also uncertain when the next "Seegfröne" will take place, if ever, because it is getting warmer in and around the lake.*

GANZ IN WEISS *All in White*

Feierlich ging es am 1. Dezember 1824 zu, als die „Wilhelm" zur ersten fahrplanmäßigen Fahrt zwischen Friedrichshafen und Rorschach aufbrach. Mit der „Wilhelm" begann die Zeit der Dampfschifffahrt auf dem Bodensee. Weitere Schiffe in Deutschland, Österreich und der Schweiz wurden in Betrieb genommen, die als „Weiße Flotte" bekannt wurden. Die „Weiße Flotte" wuchs. *Ceremonies and celebrations were the order of the day on 1st December 1824, when the "Wilhelm" set off on the first scheduled trip between Friedrichshafen and Rorschach. The "Wilhelm" heralded in the era of steam shipping on Lake Constance. Further ships came into service in Germany, Austria and Switzerland, which came to be known as the "White Fleet". The "White Fleet" grew.*

Doch der Verkehr auf Schiene und Straße war schneller und effektiver, darum schipperte die „Weiße Flotte" nun hauptsächlich für Touristen. Erst in den letzten Jahren wurden die Schiffe wieder als Verkehrsmittel entdeckt und sind auf einzelnen Strecken wieder ganzjährig in Betrieb. Die Bodensee-Fähre ist derzeit die umweltfreundlichste Verbindung zwischen Friedrichshafen und Romanshorn. Die Überfahrt zwischen Konstanz und Meersburg dauert eine erholsame Viertelstunde, die Pendler zwischen Konstanz und Meersburg zum Durchatmen nutzen. Seit 2005 sind die Städte Konstanz und Friedrichshafen durch eine direkte Katamaranlinie verbunden. Auf dem Untersee fahren mehrere Solarboote. *But rail and road transport became faster and more efficient, so that the "White Fleet" now sailed mainly for the benefit of tourists. Only in recent years have the ships been rediscovered as a viable form of transport, and on some routes are back in operation all year round. The Lake Constance Ferry is currently the most environmentally friendly connection between Friedrichshafen and Romanshorn. The crossing between Konstanz and Meersburg takes a relaxing quarter of an hour, which commuters use to take a few deep breaths between the traffic jams and stress of working life. Since 2005, the towns of Konstanz and Friedrichshafen have been connected by a direct catamaran line, and on the Untersee there are several solar-powered boats.*

Das Prachtstück der Bodenseeschifffahrt ist die „Hohentwiel". Der Schaufelraddampfer stammt aus dem Jahr 1913, er wurde restauriert und ist nun als schwimmendes Denkmal auf dem Obersee unterwegs – natürlich ganz in Weiß. *The gem amongst the shipping on Lake Constance is the "Hohentwiel", a paddle-steamer dating from the year 1913. It has been restored and now plies the Obersee as a floating monument – naturally all in white.*

ÜBERLINGER SEE

TOURISMUS UND EINSAMKEIT *TOURISM AND SOLITUDE*

Barockkirche, Pfahlbauten, Blumeninsel und das schmucke Städtchen Meersburg – alles nur wenige Kilometer voneinander entfernt. Von Bodman-Ludwigshafen bis nach Meersburg reicht der Überlinger See. Sein Hinterland gehört zu den beliebtesten Wandergebieten am See. Auf sanften Hügeln wachsen Obstbäume und Reben, langgestreckte, bewaldete Kuppen sind Zeugen der letzten Eiszeit. *Baroque church, pile constructions, island of flowers and the neat little town of Meersburg – all only a few kilometres away from each other. The Überlinger See stretches from Bodman-Ludwigshafen to Meersburg. Its hinterland is one of the most popular rambling areas on the lake. Fruit trees and vines grow on the gently rolling hills, while the elongated wooded hilltops testify to the last Ice Age.*

Meersburg ist ein Muss für Romantiker. Wobei die, zumindest in der Hochsaison, viel Geduld mitbringen sollten. Denn durch die herausgeputzten, mittelalterlichen Gassen mit den schmucken Fachwerkhäusern wollen viele bummeln. Kein Wunder, denn Meersburg liegt atemberaubend an einem steilen Hang. Das Meersburg. Seine Schlösser sieht man bei klarer Sicht sogar von den Schweizer Voralpen aus. Wie ausgestorben liegt die Stadt dagegen im Winter da. Wenn Besucher und Saisonarbeiter weg sind, promeniert man fast allein am Ufer entlang oder steigt zum Neuen Schloss empor. Dorthin, wo einst die Konstanzer Bischöfe residierten. Später diente es aber auch als Amtsgericht, als Kaserne, als Mädchenpensionat und als Schule für Gehörlose. Winterliche Einsamkeit oder sommerliche Geschäftigkeit, selbst an besucherreichen Tagen bewahrt sich Meersburg seinen Charme, diese reizvolle Mischung aus Puppenstube und der Schönheit eines Jahrhunderte lang gewachsenen Kunstwerkes. *Meersburg is a must for romantics. Although they will have to bring plenty of patience with them, especially in the peak season. Because there are many who want to stroll through the tidy medieval alleyways lined by prim, half-timbered houses. And no wonder, because Meersburg sits precariously on a steep slope. The Meersburg. In good visibility, its castles can even be seen from the foothills of the Swiss Alps. In winter however, the town looks deserted. When the visitors and seasonal workers have gone, the locals can walk almost alone along the shore or up to the "Neues Schloss" ("New Castle"), the former residence of the Bishops of Konstanz. It later also served as the District Court, a barracks, a girl's boarding school and a school for the deaf. Wintry solitude or summertime bustle, even when full of visitors, Meersburg still preserves its charm, this delightful mixture of a doll's house and the beauty of a work of art that has grown up over centuries.*

Viel früher, 4000 v. Chr., sind die Menschen am Bodensee sesshaft geworden. Sie bauten sich Häuser auf Stelzen, die Pfahlbauten. Bei Hornstadt am Untersee, bei Arbon, bei Sipplingen und am Ufer des Überlinger Sees – an fast hundert Stellen, sind Pfahlbau-Siedlungen gefunden worden, die das Wasser gut konserviert hatte. In den zwanziger Jahren des letzten Jahrhunderts ließ der damalige Bürgermeister von Uhldingen eine Pfahlbautensiedlung rekonstruieren. Die Archäologen konnten die Form der Häuser nur erahnen, denn die Erforschung der Vor- und Frühgeschichte steckte noch in den Kinderschuhen. Zudem waren die Rekonstruktionen ideologisch geprägt, denn das „Freilichtmuseum deutscher Vorzeit" sollte zeigen, wie zivilisiert unsere Vorfahren damals bereits gewesen waren. Inzwischen nehmen die Forscher an, dass sich die Siedler durch die Nähe zum Wasser vor wilden Tieren schützen wollten und der Weg zum Fischen nicht weit war. Nur vereinzelte Pfahlbauten lagen übers Wasser, die meisten Pfähle waren jedoch ins Ufer gerammt worden. 850 v. Chr. stieg der Seespiegel enorm an, die Pfahlbauten verschwanden. *People came to settle around Lake Constance much earlier, around 4,000 BC. They build houses on stilts, the pile constructions. At Hornstadt on the Untersee, at Arbon, at Sipplingen and on the bank of the Überlinger See – the remains of pile construction settlements have been found at almost 100 locations, which have been well preserved by the water. In the 1920s, the then Mayor of Uhldingen had one such settlement reconstructed. The archaeologists could only guess at the shape of the houses, because research into pre-history and early history was still in its infancy. The reconstructions also had an ideological motive: the "Freilichtmuseum deutscher Vorzeit" ("Open-air museum of German pre-history") was to show how civilised our ancestors were even at that time. Researchers now believe that the settlers chose to live so close to the water in order to protect themselves against wild animals, and to be close to their fishing grounds. Only a few isolated pile constructions lay above the water, although most piles had been driven into the banks. In 850 BC the water level in the lake rose tremendously, and the pile constructions disappeared.*

Eingebettet in Weinberge und Obstgärten, leicht erhöht am Ufer des Sees, erhebt sich eine Kirche aus dem grünen Umland: die Wallfahrtskirche Birnau. Der Blick reicht über den See mit der Insel Mainau, über das Hügelland auf der anderen Seeseite und auf das Alpenpanorama. Die Äbte von Salem, mit Hang zum Prunk, ließen die Kirche 1746 bis 1750 vom Vorarlberger Baumeister Peter Thumb bauen, ausgeschmückt hat sie Joseph Anton Feuchtmayer. Entstanden ist eine barocke Pracht aus Farben und Formen, Balustraden und Ornamenten, Erkern und Nischen. Ein opulentes Gesamtkunstwerk bis ins letzte Detail, ein Barockjuwel für die einen, blanker Kitsch für die anderen. *Nestling amongst vineyards and orchards, on a slight rise on the lake shore, a church rises up from the surrounding greenery: The Birnau "Wallfahrtskirche" ("Pilgrimage Church"). The view extends over the lake with the island of Mainau, over the hill country on the other side of the lake and on to the panorama of the Alps. The Abbots of Salem, with a tendency to pomp, had the church built in 1746 to 1750 by the Vorarlberg master builder Peter Thumb, with the interior design by Joseph Anton Feuchtmayer. The result was a piece of Baroque splendour of colours and shapes, balustrades and ornaments, oriels and niches. An opulent, cohesive masterpiece down to the last detail, a Baroque jewel to some, although plain kitsch to others.*

Überall lugen Heilige und Putten hervor, darunter auch der Putto des ungenierten Honigschleckers. Mit dem rechten Arm presst er einen Bienenkorb an sich, den linken Zeigefinger steckt er genießerisch zwischen die Lippen. Der Honigschlecker symbolisiert die Beredsamkeit des heiligen Bernhard, dem Worte wie Honig aus dem Mund geflossen sein sollen, was ihm den Beinamen „doctor mellifluus", „honigfließender Lehrer" einbrachte. *Saints and cherubs look out everywhere, including the unashamed honey-eater. With his right arm he shields a beehive against his body, the left index finger pressed appreciatively to his lips. The honey-eater symbolises the eloquence of St. Bernhard, because words are supposed to have flowed from his lips like honey, which earned him the nickname "doctor mellifluus", "honey-tongued teacher".*

Jede noch so kleine Ecke der Kirche ist reich verziert. Wer diesen Prunk sieht, kann sich kaum vorstellen, dass die Kirche nach der Säkularisierung aufgegeben worden war und zeitweise sogar als Ziegenstall gedient hat, bis sie 1919 von Zisterziensern vom Kloster Mehrerau in Bregenz wieder übernommen wurde. *Every nook and cranny of the church is richly adorned. Anyone seeing this splendour would hardly be able to believe that the church had been given up after secularisation, and for a time had even served as a stall for goats, until it was taken on again in 1919 by Cistercians from the monastery of Mehrerau in Bregenz.*

Durch all den Bombast der Kirche wird die dahinter liegende Gedenkstätte für die Opfer eines wahnwitzigen Projekts der Nationalsozialisten fast übersehen: Ganze Fabriken aus dem zerstörten Friedrichshafen sollten in den Weltkriegsjahren in den Untergrund bei Überlingen verlagert werden. Dort, im weichen Molassegestein, hatten Menschen schon vor Jahrtausenden Höhlen gegraben. Im Zweiten Weltkrieg sollten unterirdische Fabriken zur Herstellung von Waffen und Munition entstehen, dafür mussten KZ-Häftlinge aus dem Konzentrationslager Dachau unter unbeschreiblichen Bedingungen

arbeiten, viele starben. *Due to all the bombast of the church, the memorial behind it to the victims of a lunatic project of the National Socialists is almost overlooked: during the war years, whole factories from the destroyed Friedrichshafen were to be relocated underground near Überlingen. People thousands of years ago excavated caves here in the soft molasses rock. In the Second World War, underground factories were to be built for the production of arms and munitions: inmates were shipped in from the Dachau concentration camp, and many died as a result of the indescribable conditions in which they were forced to work.*

Nicht weit entfernt von Gedenkstätte und Kirche liegt Salem. Bei dem Namen denken die meisten wohl nicht an das Zisterzienserkloster, obwohl es das größte und reichste in Süddeutschland war, sondern an das berühmte Elite-Internat. Prinz Max von Baden und der Pädagoge Kurt Hahn gründeten die Schule 1920, die im Westflügel des Schlosses untergebracht ist. „Das Schlimmste für mich als Stadtkind war, dass ich mich um die Hühner kümmern musste. Ein Mal pro Woche musste ich sogar ausmisten", erinnerte sich die Politikerin Hildegard Hamm-Brücher an ihre Salemer Zeit. Auch Theodor Heuss, der erste Präsident der Bundesrepublik, der Schriftsteller Golo Mann und die spanische Königin Sophia drückten hier die Schulbank, ebenso Prinz Philip, Gemahl der englischen Königin Elisabeth II. *Not far from the memorial and the church lies Salem. Most people probably associate the name not with the Cistercian monastery, although it was the largest and wealthiest in southern Germany, but rather with*

the famous elite boarding school. Prince Max of Baden and the educationalist Kurt Hahn founded the school, which is accommodated in the west wing of the castle, in 1920. "The worst thing of all for me as a 'townie' was that I had to look after the chickens. I even had to muck them out once a week", recalled the politician Hildegard Hamm-Brücher of her time at Salem. The school was also attended by Theodor Heuss, the first President of the Federal Republic, the author Golo Mann and the Spanish Queen Sophia, as well as Prince Philip, the consort of the British Queen Elisabeth II.

Namensgeber für den Überlinger See ist seine größte Stadt, die auch den Beinamen „badisches Nizza" trägt. Wein, Getreide und Salz legten einst den Grundstock für Überlingens Reichtum, fünf Millionen Liter Wein wurden im Jahr 1597 gekeltert. Die starke Stellung der Weinbauern bescherte ihnen schon im Mittelalter Sitze in der Stadtregierung. Der Dreißigjährige Krieg ruinierte Überlingen. Erst fielen die Schweden 1632 ein, zwei Jahre später belagerten sie die Stadt. „Frauen und Kinder zum Beten, die Männer zum Kämpfen", war der Befehl während der Belagerung. „Wenn die Schweden endlich abziehen, dann werden wir für alle Ewigkeit eine feierliche Prozession halten", versprachen die Überlinger. Und tatsächlich: Sobald die Schweden abgezogen waren, lösten die Überlinger ihr Versprechen ein. In einer feierlichen Prozession zogen Geistliche, Stadtväter, Bürgerinnen und Bürger von Kirchenaltar zu Kirchenaltar, samt „Schwedenmadonna" und anderen Kostbarkeiten aus der Schatzkammer des Münsters St. Nikolaus. Bis heute gilt das Versprechen, jedes Jahr im Mai und Juli gibt es eine Schwedenprozession. *The Überlinger See is named after its largest town, which also boasts the nickname the "Nice of Baden". Wine, corn and salt laid the initial foundations for Überlingen's wealth, with 5 million litres of wine being produced in the year 1597. The strong position of the wine-growers ensured them of seats on the Town Council. But Überlingen was devastated by the Thirty Years War. The first to arrive were the Swedish in 1632, and two years later they laid siege to the town. "Women and children to praying, the men to fighting", was the command during the siege. "When the Swedish finally withdraw, we will hold a ceremonial procession forevermore", promised the people of Überlingen. And as soon as the Swedish had withdrawn, they kept their promise. Clerics, city fathers and citizen made a ceremonial procession from church altar to church altar, carrying the "Schwedenmadonna" and other precious objects from the treasury of the Minster of St. Nikolaus. The promise continues to be upheld today, and the "Sweden Procession" takes place every year in May and July.*

Dichter Wald, Moos, felsige, steil abfallende Ufer, wildromantisch zeigt sich der Bodanrück auf der Westseite des Überlinger Sees. Mit Flurnamen wie Teufelsstich und Teufelstal. Und einer grandiosen Schlucht. Tief hat sich ein Bach durchs Gestein gegraben und die Marienschlucht geschaffen. Ein verschlungener, enger Pfad führt durch die Klamm, von 30 Meter hohen Felswänden umgeben, unter Holztreppen gurgelt der Bach. Einst, als die Schlucht noch keinen Namen trug, wurde sie zum Verlobungspräsent. Graf zu Bodman schenkte die Schlucht seiner Marie, die ihr dann ihren Namen gab. Kalt, schattig und ruhig ist es am Nachmittag in der Schlucht. Einsam fast. *Dense forest, moss, rocky, steeply shelving banks, this is the wild and romantic "Bodanrück" ("Bodan ridge") on the west side of the Überlinger See. With place names such as the "Teufelsstich" ("Devil's thrust") and "Teufelstal" ("Devil's vale"). And an impressive gorge. Here a stream has worn its way deep through the rock to form the "Marienschlucht". A narrow, winding path leads through the ravine, surrounded by 100ft. high rock walls, with the stream gurgling away under the wooden stairs. Once, before the gorge had any name, it became an engagement present. The Count of Bodman presented it to his Marie, who then named it after herself. The afternoon in the gorge is cool, calm and shady. Lonely almost.*

Mit flatterndem Haar vor dem Fürstenhäusle *With Fluttering Hair Before the Prince's Chalet*

Auf der Burg haus' ich am Berge,
unter mir der blaue See,
höre nächtlich Koboldzwerge,
täglich Adler in der Höh'.

I lodge in the castle on the mountain,
below me lies the blue lake,
nightly hear the goblins stirring,
daily eagles in the heights.

Im September 1841 besucht Annette von Droste-Hülshoff (1797 – 1848) ihre Schwester Jenny und ihren Schwager Joseph Freiherr von Laßberg, der das Schloss Meersburg gekauft hatte. Das milde Klima am See gefällt ihr besser als der westfälische Dauerregen. Sie bleibt ein ganzes Jahr auf dem Schloss, kauft sich dann ein Haus in Meersburg, das Fürstenhäusle. Von dort blickt die Dichterin auf den See hinab, dessen wechselnde Stimmungen sie über alles liebt. Dort lässt sie den Sturm im „flatternden Haar" wühlen. *In September 1841, Annette von Droste-Hülshoff (1797 – 1848) visited her sister Jenny and her brother-in-law Joseph Freiherr von Laßberg, who had bought the castle at Meersburg. She found the mild climate of the lake much more to her taste than the permanent rain of Westphalia. She stayed at the castle for a whole year, before buying herself a house in Meersburg, the "Prince's Chalet". From here the poetess gazed down on the lake, whose changing moods she loved above all else. Here she let the storm blow through her "fluttering hair".*

Vermutlich verbringt sie in Meersburg die schönsten Momente ihres Lebens. Als nämlich ihr um 17 Jahre jüngerer Freund, der Dichter Levin Schücking, als Bibliothekar im Schloss weilt, Droste-Hülshoff ist von Schücking mehr als angetan, allerdings ist bis heute unklar, wie weit dies in den Konventionen des Biedermeiers ging. Jedenfalls inspiriert Schücking die Dichterin und hilft ihr durch seine guten Kontakte. So finden ihre Gedichte einen Verleger. „Am Bodensee", „Der Säntis", „Am Turme", „Das alte Schloß" – Gedichte, in denen die enge Beziehung zu ihrer neuen Heimat zum Ausdruck bringt. Manchmal setzt sie ihr sogar ein kritisches und spöttisches literarisches Denkmal. *Perhaps she spent the most beautiful moments of her life here in Meersburg, when her friend, the poet Levin Schücking, her junior by 17 years, worked for a time as the castle librarian. Droste-Hülshoff was more than fond of Schücking, although it is still not clear today how far this went in the Biedermeier conventions. In any case Schücking inspired the poetess, and helped her with his good contacts. Her poems therefore found a publisher. "Am Bodensee", "Der Säntis", "Am Turme", "Das alte Schloß" – poems in which the Westphalian expresses her close relationship with her new home, sometimes even creating a critical and facetious literary monument to it.*

Bei ihrem Schwager treffen sich Gelehrte und Schriftsteller. Gustav Schwab ist dabei und Ludwig Uhland. Doch die Droste tut die Herren ab als „langweilig wie der bittre Tod". Dieser ereilt sie am 24. Mai 1848, beigesetzt ist sie auf dem Meersburger Friedhof. *Academics and writers met under her brother-in-law's roof, Gustav Schwab was there and Ludwig Uhland. But Droste shrugged them off as "boring as death". This came to her on 24th May 1848, and she now lies in the cemetery at Meersburg.*

Ein Fest für die Augen *A Feast for the Eyes*

Wenn die Kirschen blühen, sollen sich unter den Zweigen farblich abgestimmte Tulpenkelche öffnen. Hornveilchen, Begonien, Mohn und Hibiskus blühen. Rosen folgen auf Rhododendron, und Dahlien sorgen für ein herbstliches Finale. Nichts auf der Insel Mainau bleibt dem Zufall überlassen. Egal, ob

Ostern früh im Jahr ist oder später, wenn die Osterbesucher kommen, müssen Osterglocken und Tulpen blühen. Der Beiname „Blumeninsel" verpflichtet. *When the cherry trees blossom, matching tulip calyxes are said to open under the branches. Tufted pansies, begonias, poppies and hibiscus blossom. Roses follow rhododendrons, and dahlias provide the autumn finale. Nothing on the island of Mainau is left to chance. Whether Easter comes early in the year or later, when the Easter visitors come, the daffodils and tulips must be in bloom. The obligation imposed by the nickname "Blumeninsel" ("Island of flowers").*

Feuchtwarme Luft legt sich schwer auf die Haut, Wasser plätschert, Grün, nichts als Grün und ein lautloses Flattern überall. Schmetterlinge, manche groß wie Spatzen und bunt wie Papageien, manche winzig mit transparenten Flügeln, andere glänzen metallisch. Exotische Vielfalt. Alle flattern sie im Schmetterlingshaus der Mainau. *Moist warm air lies heavily on the skin, the gentle splashing of water, green, nothing but green and an almost soundless fluttering everywhere. Butterflies, some as large as sparrows and as brightly coloured as parrots, some tiny with transparent wings, others gleaming like metallic shards, floating on the warm air. The exotic variety of the butterfly house on Mainau.*

Seit 1271 war die Insel ein wichtiger Stützpunkt des Deutschen Ordens. Erst 1853 gelangte die Mainau an den Großherzog Friedrich I. von Baden. Von ihm stammen die Zedern und Mammutbäume, die er im „Arboretum" pflanzen ließ. Friedrichs Tochter Viktoria wurde schwedische Königin und vererbte die Insel ihrem Enkel, Lennart Graf Bernadotte. Eigentlich sollte er schwedischer König werden, doch seine Hochzeit mit einer Bürgerlichen schloss ihn von der Thronfolge aus. Der Graf zog auf die Mainau und machte aus ihr ein Blumenparadies, das zu einer der bedeutendsten Touristenattraktionen am Bodensee wurde. Im Zweiten Weltkrieg diente die Insel der NS-Organisation Todt als Sitz. Nach Kriegsende erholten sich hier ehemalige französische KZ-Häftlinge. *Since 1271, the island had been an important centre of the Teutonic Order. Not until 1853 did Mainau pass to the Grand Duke Friedrich I of Baden. From him come the cedars and sequoias which he had planted in his "Arboretum". Friedrich's daughter Victoria became the Queen of Sweden, and bequeathed the island to her grandson, Lennart Count Bernadotte. He should have become the King of Sweden, but his marriage to a commoner excluded him from succession to the throne. The Count removed to Mainau, turning it into a paradise of flowers which became one of the major tourist attractions on Lake Constance. In the Second World War, the island was used as the headquarters of the National Socialist Todt Organisation. After the end of the war, French former concentration camp inmates were brought here to recover.*

2001 wird Sonja Gräfin Bernadotte alleinige Geschäftsführerin der Mainau. 2005 stirbt 96-jährig ihr Gatte, im Oktober 2008 stirbt sie selbst. Seit Anfang 2007 ist die Tochter der beiden, Bettina Gräfin Bernadotte, die Geschäftsführerin des Mainau-Unternehmens mit Park, Tiergehege, Streichelzoo und Schaubauernhof. *In 2001, Sonja Countess Bernadotte became the sole director of Mainau. Her husband died in 2005 at the age of 96, and she herself died in October 2008. Since the beginning of 2007, their daughter, Bettina Countess Bernadotte, has been the director of the Mainau company, with its park, animal enclosures, petting zoo and show farm.*

An der Auffahrt zur Insel steht das „Schwedenkreuz". Die bronzene Kreuzigungsgruppe aus dem Jahr 1577 wurde von den Schweden während des Dreißigjährigen Kriegs aus dem Kloster entwendet. Doch den Soldaten war die Kriegsbeute zu schwer, deshalb versenkten sie sie kurzerhand im See. Palmenhaus, Ausstellungen, Schmetterlinge und Blütenpracht die Mainau ist ein Fest für die Augen. *At the approach to the island stands the "Schwedenkreuz" ("Swedish Cross"). The bronze trio of crucifixions dating from the year 1577 was stolen from the monastery by the Swedish during the Thirty Years War. But this war booty proved to be too heavy for the soldiers, so they simply threw it into the lake. The Palm House, exhibitions, butterflies and the magnificent flowerbeds – Mainau is truly a feast for the eyes.*

Neue Heimat im Biotop *A New Home in the Biotope*

Der Biotopverbund Bodensee wächst. Zwischen Stockach, Meersburg und Pfullendorf, auf einer Fläche von 350 Quadratkilometern, entsteht ein Verbund von mehr als hundert Biotopen. Dadurch soll bedrohten Tieren und Pflanzen eine Rückzugsmöglichkeit geboten und die gesamte Artenvielfalt vergrößert werden. Angefangen hat alles im Sommer 2005 mit dem Billafinger Weiher. Mit Hilfe von Baggern und einer Finanzspritze der Heinz-Sielmann-Stiftung wurde aus einer Feuchtwiese ein Weiher. Hatten Vogelkundler vor der Renaturierung dort 115 Vogelarten gezählt, so sind es mittlerweile mehr als 160. Auch Bisam, Iltis und Hermelin leben nun am Weiher. Im See schwimmen über 100.000 Fische, und am Ufer wachsen 230 seltene Stauden, Kräuter und Sträucher. Durch den Biotopenverbund Bodensee werden die Bäche aus ihren Betonbetten geholt, Streuobstwiesen gepflanzt, Flachmoorwiesen vernässt und Naturschutz aus ehemaligen Tongruben entstehen Teiche. Neuer Lebensraum wird geschaffen und praktiziert. *The "Biotopverbund Bodensee" ("Lake Constance Biotope Society") is growing. Between Stockach, Meersburg and Pfullendorf, on an area of 350 km², an association of over 100 biotopes is being created. This is intended to provide a refuge for threatened animals and plants, and increase the overall variety of species. It all began in the summer of 2005 with the "Billafinger Weiher". With the aid of excavators and a cash injection from the Heinz-Sielmann Foundation, a water meadow was turned into a man-made lake. Before this return to nature, ornithologists had counted 115 species of birds here: the number has now increased to over 160. Muskrat, polecat and ermine have now returned to the area. The lake holds over 100,000 fish, and 230 varieties of rare shrubs, herbs and bushes now grow along the banks. The Biotopverbund Bodensee has rescued streams from the restrictions of their concrete beds, planted fruit meadows and irrigated dry moorland meadows: claypits are being turned into ponds, creating a new habitat for wildlife – real nature conservation in practice.*

Provokateur am Bodensee *A Provocateur on Lake Constance*

Schalk vom Bodensee wird er genannt, manchmal auch moderner Till Eulenspiegel. Peter Lenk provoziert. Seine Kunst polarisiert. Er verletzt Tabus. Und er ist einer der begehrtesten zeitgenössischen Bildhauer: Peter Lenk, 1947 in Nürnberg geboren. *"Schalk vom Bodensee" he is called, and sometimes also the modern Till Eulenspiegel. Peter Lenk is a provocateur. His art is polarising. He eagerly violates taboos. And he is one of the most sought-after contemporary sculptors: Peter Lenk, born in Nürnberg in 1947.*

„Peter Lenk vergrämt mit einer riesigen Plastik die katholische Geistlichkeit", war 1993 im Nachrichtenmagazin „Der Spiegel" zu lesen. Im Konstanzer Hafen, umweht vom warmen Südwind, steht der Anlass: Imperia, neun Meter hoch, fünfzehn Tonnen schwer, sehr freizügig gekleidet, üppige Kurven und auf ihren Handflächen trägt sie zwei kümmerliche Witzgestalten. Vielleicht hätte diese Statue die Geistlichkeit gar nicht gekümmert, wäre Imperia nicht eine „Hübschlerin", eine Edelhure aus dem 15. Jahrhundert gewesen, die „Keuschheitsgelübde in Liebessehnen" verwandelt haben soll. Ausgerechnet Imperia trägt auf den emporgehaltenen Händen zwei Gaukler, wie Lenk sie nennt. Besagte Gaukler haben eine verblüffende Ähnlichkeit mit Papst Martin V. und Kaiser Sigismund. Das war zu viel. Geschmacklos und geeignet, den religiösen Frieden zu beeinträchtigen! Unmoralisch! Frauenfeindlich! Ein Hurendenkmal! Der Bodmaner Künstler Lenk wurde mit Beschimpfungen überschüttet. Der Konstanzer Gemeinderat beschloss, Imperia müsse weichen. Doch die Statue steht nicht auf städtischem Grund, darum hatte der Rat keine Handhabe. Die Konstanzer wollten Imperia behalten. Die hatte von 1455 bis 1511 tatsächlich gelebt, allerdings in Rom. Nach Konstanz verpflanzte sie Honoré de Balzac literarisch in seinen „Tolldreisten Geschichten". *"Peter Lenk offends Catholic spirituality with this mound of plastic", as was written in 1993 in the news magazine "Der Spiegel". In the harbour of Konstanz, caressed by the warm south wind, stands the reason: Imperia, nine metres high, weighing fifteen tonnes, very revealingly dressed, with voluptuous curves, and carrying on the palms of her hands two small comic figures. Perhaps this statue would not have offended spirituality if Imperia were not a "Hübschlerin", a high-class prostitute of the 15th Century, who is supposed to have transformed the "vow of chastity into a yearning for love". Imperia carries on her upheld hands two imposters, as Lenk calls them. These imposters bear an uncanny resemblance to Pope Martin V and Emperor Sigismund. This was too much. Tasteless and likely to arouse religious conflict! Immoral! Anti-feminist! A monument to a whore! The Bodman artist Lenk was showered with insults and criticism. The Konstanz Town Council decided that Imperia would have to go. But the statue is not standing on municipal property, so the Council had no power to act. The people of Konstanz wanted to keep Imperia. She did actually live from 1455 to 1511, although in Rome. She was transplanted to Konstanz in literature by Honoré de Balzac in his "Les contes drolatiques".*

Nach dem Studium an der Kunstakademie in Stuttgart hatte es Peter Lenk an den Bodensee gezogen, wo er in Bodman heimisch wurde. Die „Magische Säule" an der Hafenmole in Meersburg, die „Dix-Kurve" in Gaienhofen und in Überlingen die drei Werke „Prominente und Proleten", „Napoleondenkmal" und der „Bodenseereiter" – der Bodmaner ist mit seiner Kunst in seiner Region präsent. „Bodenseereiter" heißt der Brunnen, der direkt am See alle Blicke auf sich zieht. Der Künstler hat dem matten Reiter die Züge des Schriftstellers Martin Walser verpasst und ihm mit Schlittschuhen statt Sporen auf einen müden Esel gesetzt. Von hängebrüstigen Nixen gestützt trottet der Esel dahin, einen Ritt über den Bodensee imitierend. Der Eklat war perfekt. Peter Lenk provoziert. *After studying at the Academy of Art in Stuttgart, Peter Lenk was drawn to Lake Constance, where he took up residence in Bodman. The "Magische Säule" on the harbour mole in Meersburg, the "Dix-Kurve" in Gaienhofen and in Überlingen the three works "Prominente und Proleten", "Napoleondenkmal" and the "Bodenseereiter" – Lenk is present throughout the region with his art. "Bodenseereiter" is also the name of the fountain right on the lake which attracts everyone's attention. The artist has given the rider the features of the author Martin Walser, seating him on a tired old nag, and wearing skates instead of spurs. Supported by mermaids with sagging breasts, the horse trots on, imitating the ride over Lake Constance. The éclat was perfect. Peter Lenk is a provocateur.*

Meersburg liegt wie eine Aussichtsterrasse am nördlichen Bodenseeufer. Weit reicht der Blick über die Insel Mainau und den Bodanrück bis hinein ins Schweizer Alpenmassiv. Das Städtchen ist von Weinbergen umgeben.

Meersburg sits like an observation terrace on the northern shore of Lake Constance. The view ranges far and wide over the island of Mainau and the "Bodanrück" to the massif of the Swiss Alps. The village is surrounded by vineyards.

20

Bedrohlich ziehen abendliche Sommergewitter übers Wasser heran. Jetzt halten die Meersburger Weinbauern den Atem an.

Evening summer storms approach threateningly over the water. At times like this, the Meersburg wine-growers can only hold their breath and hope for the best.

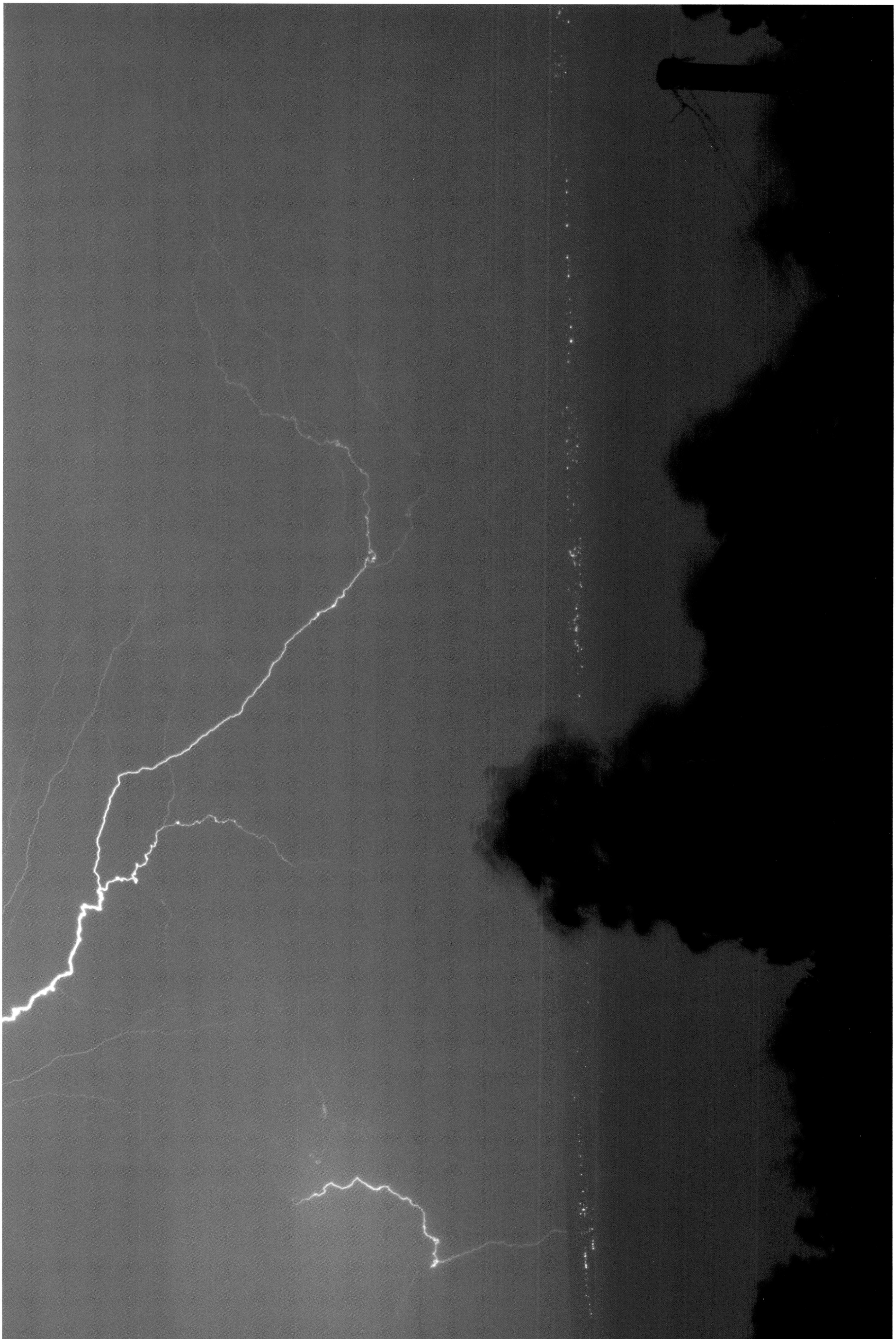

In gleichmäßigen Bahnen verteilen sich Föhnwolken über den Himmel. Vor dieser Naturkulisse erscheint Meersburg sogar noch schöner.

Föhn clouds march in even lines across the sky. Against this natural backdrop, Meersburg looks even more beautiful.

Mit den ersten Nebeln des Herbstes versiegen die Besucherströme des Sommers. Jetzt ist eine gute Zeit für ausgedehnte, einsame Spaziergänge durch die Weinberge.

With the first mists of autumn, the flood of summer visitors dries up. Now is the time for long, lonely walks through the vineyards.

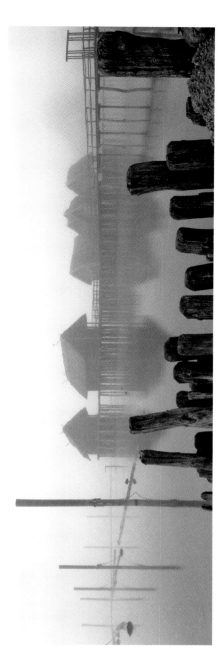

Die Unteruhldinger Pfahlbauten. Vor rund 3.000 Jahren, in der Bronzezeit, haben sich hier Siedler am Bodenseeufer niedergelassen. In den 1920er Jahren hat man ihr Dorf rekonstruiert.

The pile constructions at Unteruhldingen. People arrived here to settle on the shore of Lake Constance around 3.000 years ago, in the Bronze Age. Their village was reconstructed in the 1920's.

Die Wallfahrtskirche Birnau. Sie wurde im 18. Jahrhundert von Baumeister Peter Thumb erbaut und ist eines der vielen Kleinode barocker Baukunst am See.

The "Wallfahrtskirche" at Birnau. Built in the 18ᵗʰ Century by master builder Peter Thumb, it is one of the many jewels of Baroque architecture on the lake.

Die ehemals freie Reichsstadt Überlingen blickt auf eine stolze, über 1.200-jährige Geschichte zurück. Mit ihrem gut erhaltenen, historischen Ortskern und der längsten Promenade am See zeigt die Stadt in der Blütenpracht des Frühlings ihr schönstes Gesicht.

The former free imperial town of Überlingen can look back on a proud history of over 1,200 years. With its well-preserved historic town centre, and the longest promenade on the lake, the town shows itself to best advantage amidst the splendour of spring blossoms.

Vom Museumsgarten aus lässt sich die Überlinger Altstadt mit Münster und Pfennigturm überblicken. Der kleine Pavillon im Vordergrund ist ein beliebtes Fotomotiv bei Hochzeitsgesellschaften.

The museum garden offers an enchanting view of the Überlingen old town with its Minster and the "Pfennigturm". The small pavilion in the foreground is a popular photographic setting for wedding parties.

32

Um Überlingen herum ist die Landschaft vom Weinbau geprägt, wie hier zwischen Goldbach und Hödingen, gleich oberhalb des Natur-denkmals „Gletschermühle".

The landscape around Überlingen is characterised by wine-growing, as here between Goldbach and Hödingen, directly above the natural monument of the "Gletschermühle".

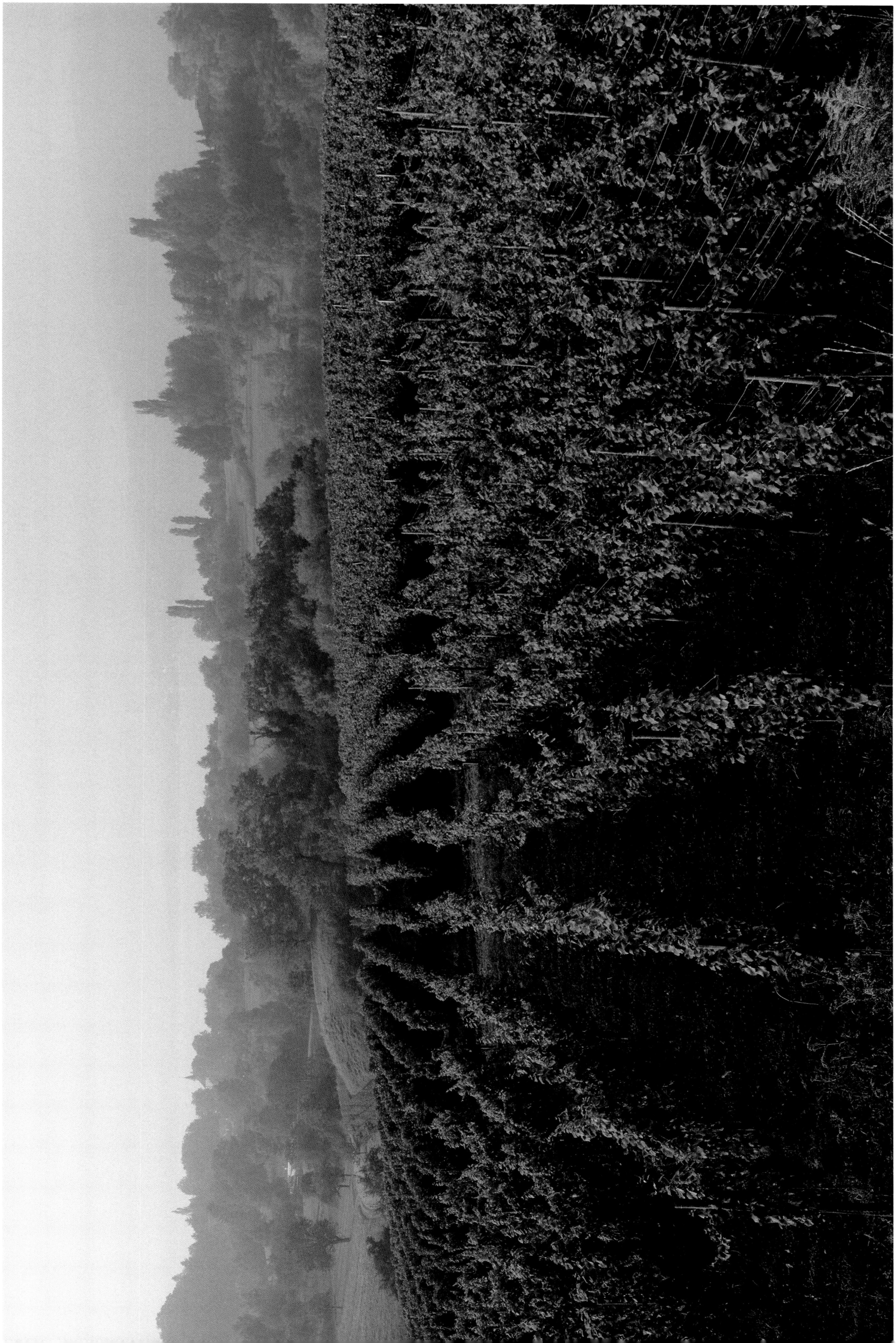

34

An warmen Sommertagen ziehen häufig Gewitterfronten aus Richtung Hegau auf. Jetzt müssen die Wassersportler auf der Hut sein, denn schnell wird aus dem eben noch beschaulich daliegenden Gewässer ein ungestümer Gegner.

On warm summer days, weather fronts frequently approach from the direction of Hegau. Water sports enthusiasts must now be on their guard, because the still calm waters can quickly become a stormy adversary.

Vom „Otto-Hagg-Weg" aus bietet sich ein prächtiger Ausblick auf Sipplingen. Hier kann der Wanderer verschnaufen, bevor er sich zur nächsten Etappe der Besteigung des „Sipplinger Bergs" aufmacht.

The splendid outlook from the "Otto-Hagg-Weg" over Sipplingen. Ramblers can pause here for breath before tackling the next stage of the "Sipplinger Berg".

Nur noch die Kirchturmspitze lässt Sipplingen erahnen. Wie eine Glocke hängt die Herbstfeuchtigkeit über dem See.

Only the church spire shows where Sipplingen lies under the blanket of autumn mist shrouding the lake.

Der Nebel verwandelt das Sipplinger Ufer in eine Geisterlandschaft, denn er nimmt dem Auge die gewohnten Bezugspunkte.

The mist turns the Sipplingen shore into a ghostly landscape, concealing from the eyes all the usual reference points.

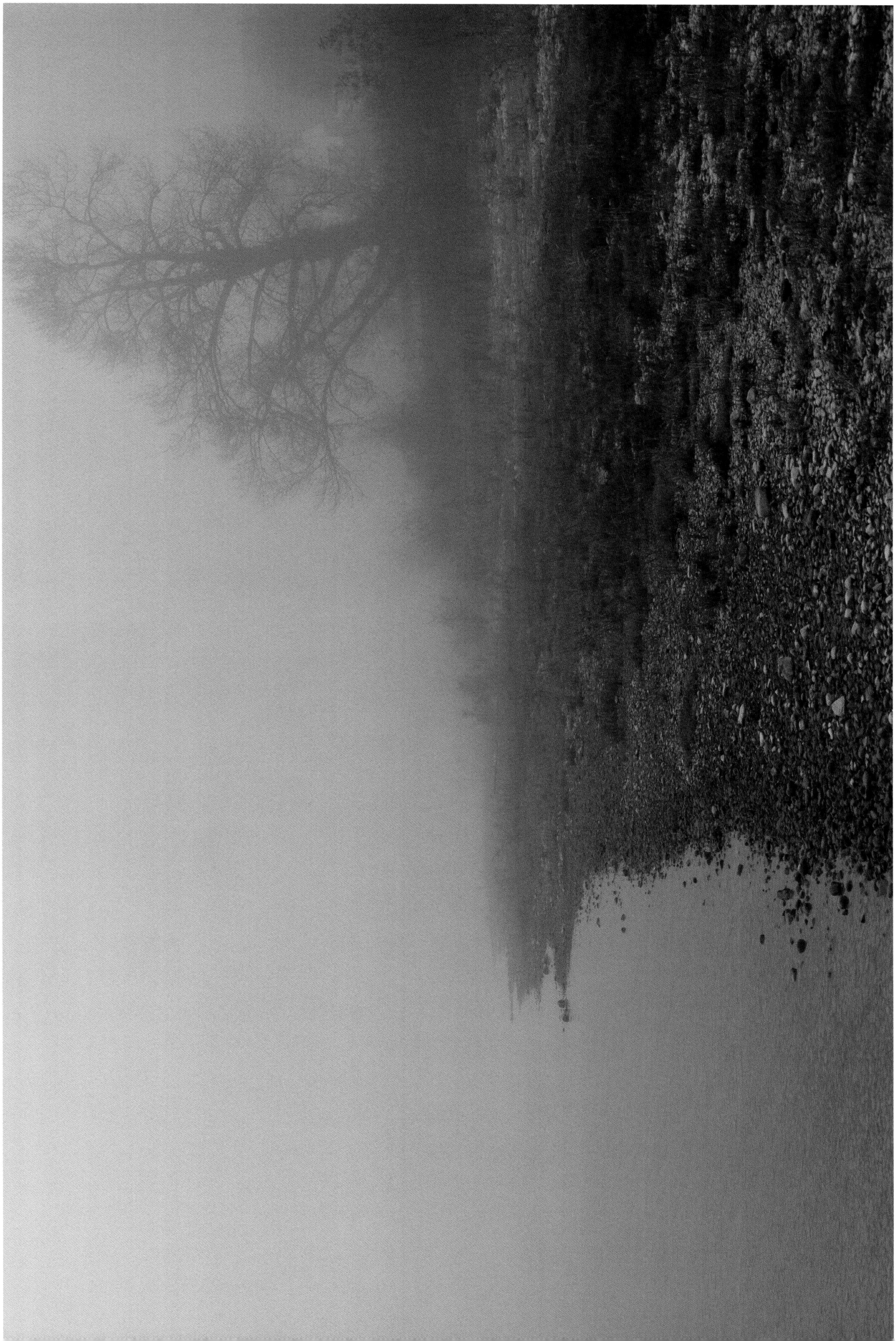

Das Aachried zwischen Ludwigshafen und Bodman im ersten Licht des neuen Tages. Das 130 Hektar große Naturschutzgebiet ist ein Refugium für zahlreiche Vogelarten, darunter Zwergtaucher, Eisvogel, Nachtigall und Teichrohrsänger.

The "Aachried" between Ludwigshafen and Bodman in the first light of the new day. This 320-acre nature preservation area provides a refuge for many species of birds, including little grebes, kingfishers, nightingales and reed warblers.

Das Seeufer zwischen Bodman und Ludwigshafen. Die landwirtschaftlich genutzten Wiesen am Rande des Aachrieds sind von Silberweiden gesäumt, die in Wassernähe wachsen.

The lake shore between Bodman and Ludwigshafen. The cultivated meadows at the edge of the "Aachried" are fringed by white willows, which grow close to the water.

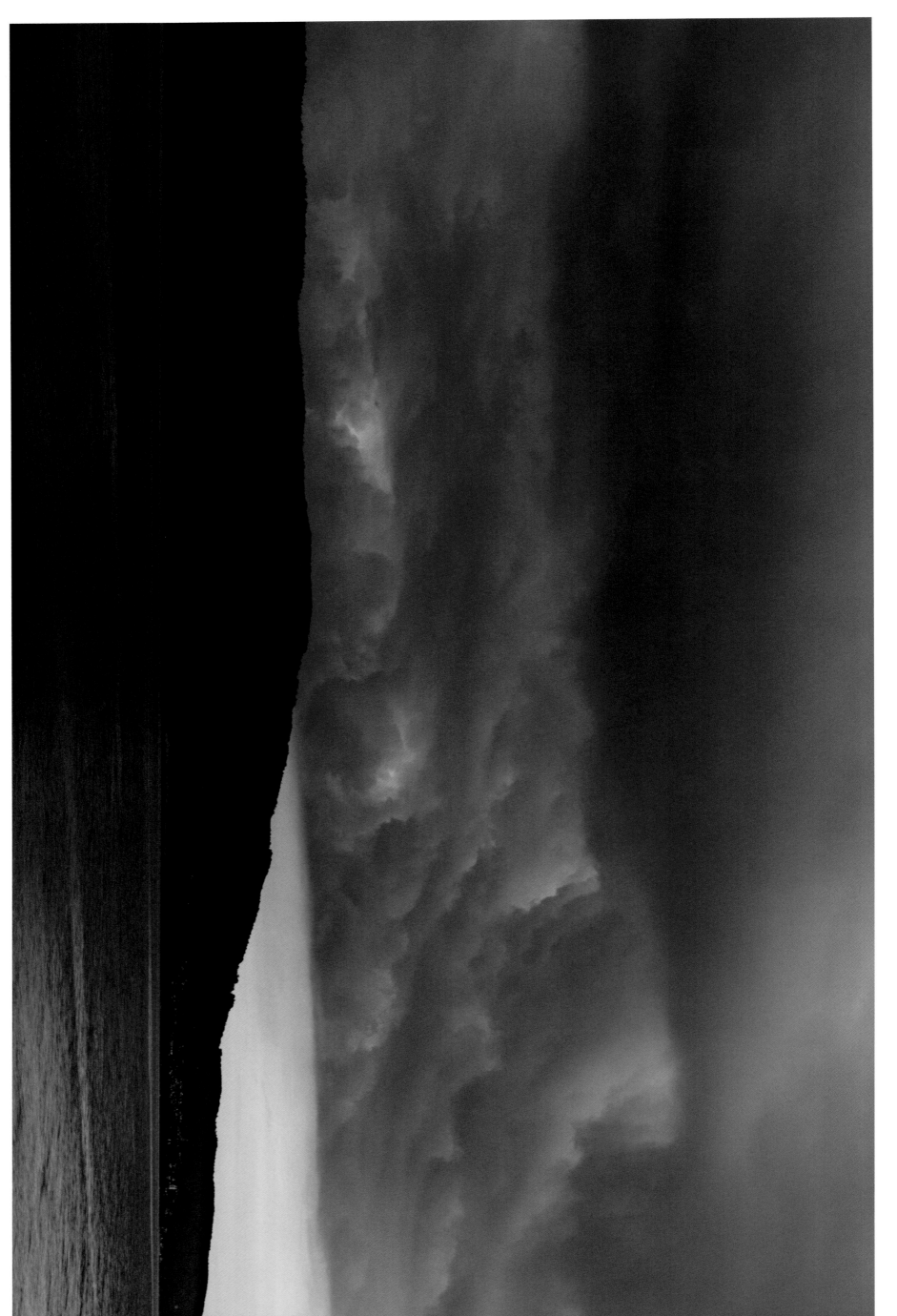

Dunkel und bedrohlich schiebt sich eine Gewitterfront bei Bodman über den See. Bald werden die ersten Blitze zucken und schon ist heftiger Wind aufgekommen. Surfer und Segler sollten jetzt lieber an Land bleiben.

Dark and threatening, a weather front sweeps over the lake at Bodman. Soon the first flashes of lightning will be seen as the wind increases in force. Surfers and sailors would now be well-advised to stay on land.

46

Eine Sonnenfinsternis über der Uferlandschaft des Bodanrücks bei Wallhausen. Es ist fünf Uhr morgens, Nebelbänke schieben sich vor die aufgehende Sonne und erleichtern das Beobachten dieses Naturereignisses.

A solar eclipse over the shore landscape of the "Bodanrück" at Wallhausen. It is five o'clock in the morning, as banks of mist soften the glare of the rising sun, making it easier to observe this natural phenomenon.

Dingelsdorf. Frühlingsidylle am Ortsrand.

Dingelsdorf. A spring idyll on the edge of the village.

Seltsame Eisformationen haben die Wellen an diesem kalten Wintermorgen entlang des Litzelstettener Ufers aufgetürmt, während sich im Hintergrund die erste Sonne über der im Winterschlaf liegenden Insel Mainau zeigt.

On this cold morning, the waves have piled up strange ice formations along the Litzelstetten shore, while in the background, the first sun reveals itself over the island of Mainau lying in winter sleep.

Die in den See ragende, kleine Landspitze von Klausenhorn zwischen Dingelsdorf und Wallhausen war früher die sicherste Schiffsanlegestelle für Überquerungen des Bodensees. Sie war und ist auch ein Wallfahrtsort der Pilger auf dem Jakobsweg.

The small headland of Klausenhorn projecting into the lake between Dingelsdorf and Wallhausen was earlier the safest mooring for crossing Lake Constance. It still remains a place of pilgrimage for those following the "Jakobsweg".

Noch erstrahlt die Landschaft vor der Insel Mainau im sommerlichen Licht, doch am Himmel braut sich schon ein Unwetter zusammen.

The landscape before the island of Mainau is still brilliant in the summer light, but in the sky, a storm is brewing.

An Sommertagen wie diesem schwebt ein betörender Duft über dem „italienischen Rosengarten" der Blumeninsel Mainau.

On summer days like this, a heady scent hangs over the "Italian rose garden" of the flower island of Mainau.

UNTERSEE

LIEBLICH UND ÜBERSCHAUBAR *COSY AND MANAGEABLE*

Der Untersee ist nur durch ein Nadelöhr mit dem Obersee verbunden. Zwischen dem Konstanzer Ortsteil Paradies und Kreuzlingen fließt der Rhein als einzige Verbindung, ehe sich hinter dem Schweizer Ort Gottlieben der Untersee öffnet. In einer der Rückzugsphasen des Rheingletschers entstanden, plätscherten am Untersee schon Wellen, als der gesamte Obersee noch unter einer dicken Eisschicht lag.

Der Untersee ist seicht, das andere Ufer immer zum Greifen nah, nie wird die Weite erreicht, die dem Obersee den Namen „Schwäbisches Meer" verlieh. Lieblich ist die Landschaft. Überschaubar.

The Untersee is connected to the Obersee only by a narrow passage. Between the Konstanz district of Paradies and Kreuzlingen flows the Rhein, forming the only connection, before the Untersee opens up behind the Swiss village of Gottlieben. Created by one of the withdrawal phases of the Rhein glacier, waves were already lapping on the Untersee when the whole Obersee still lay under a thick sheet of ice. The Untersee is shallow, the opposite shore almost close enough to touch, never achieving the sense of space and distance which gave the Obersee the name of the "Swabian Sea". Here the landscape is cosier, more manageable.

Zwischen der Mettnau vor Radolfzell und der Halbinsel Höri liegt der Zellersee. Der Seeanteil zwischen Reichenau und dem Bodanrück heißt Gnadensee. Der Name geht auf die Zeit zurück, als auf der Reichenau, der „Insel der Seligen", das Waffentragen verboten war. Zum Tode Verurteilte wurden im gegenüberliegenden Allensbach hingerichtet. Bei weniger schweren Verbrechen stand es dem Reichenauer Abt frei, den Verurteilten zu begnadigen. Dann läutete das Armesünderglöcklein, und der Verurteilte wurde in Allensbach freigelassen.

Between the Mettnau before Radolfzell and the Höri peninsula lies the Zellersee. The part of the lake between Reichenau and the Bodan Ridge is called the "Gnadensee" ("Lake of Mercy"). The name goes back to the time when the bearing of arms was forbidden on Reichenau, the "island of the blessed". Those sentenced to death were executed in Allensbach on the opposite shore. For less serious crimes, the Abbot of Reichenau was empowered to pardon the convicted person. The "Armesünderglöcklein" ("poor sinners' bell") was then rung, and the offender was released in Allensbach.

Die heimliche Hauptstadt der gesamten Bodenseeregion ist Konstanz, zumal es zusammen mit den Schweizer Nachbarorten die größte zusammenhängende Ansiedlung am Bodensee ist. Konstanz schaffte es, Taufpate für den See zu werden, zumindest im angelsächsischen und französischen Sprachraum. „Lake Constance" heißt der Bodensee auf Englisch, „Lac de Constance" auf Französisch.

Konstanz, especially since together with the neighbouring Swiss towns it makes up the largest contiguous settlement on Lake Constance. Konstanz succeeded in passing its name on to the lake, at least in English and French – the "Bodensee" in German, "Lake Constance" in English, "Lac de Constance" in French.

Der milde Seewind streichelt die Wasseroberfläche, in den Straßencafés sind freie Plätze rar. In Konstanz herrscht mediterrane Leichtigkeit, die Nähe zur Schweiz und zu Italien verstärkt den Eindruck. Fassadenmalereien an den Häusern der Altstadtgassen erzählen die Geschichte der Stadt: Auf den Böden eines einstigen Römerkastells wurde im 6. Jahrhundert die Bischofskirche gebaut. Im „Haus zur Kunkel" schildern die Fresken die Frauen, die Leinen und Seide webten. Konstanz war im Hochmittelalter ein Zentrum der Weberei.

The gentle lake breeze caresses the surface of the water, in the pavement cafés empty seats are rare. In Konstanz an atmosphere of Mediterranean lightness reigns, the impression only being strengthened by the proximity to Switzerland and Italy. Façade paintings on the houses lining the narrow streets of the old town recount the history of the town: the "Bischofskirche" ("Bishop's Church") was built in the 6th Century on the site of a former Roman fort. In the "Haus zur Kunkel", the frescoes depict the daily life of the women, who wove linen and silk. Konstanz was a centre of weaving in the late Middle Ages.

Als die Bischofskirche 1052 einstürzte, wurde auf dem Gelände bis 1089 das romanische Münster Unserer Lieben Frau gebaut, im 14. und 15. Jahrhundert wurde es gotisch, später barock umgestaltet. Lange hatten alamannische Herzöge, herüberblickend von der Burg auf dem Hohentwiel, die Stadt fest im Griff. Erst als Konstanz freie Reichsstadt wurde, entwickelte sich das Selbstbewusstsein der Bürger.

When the Bischofskirche collapsed in 1052, it was replaced by the Minster of "Unserer Lieben Frau", completed in 1089, in the 14th and 15th Century it was redesigned in the Gothic style, and later in the Baroque style. For a long time the town was firmly in the grip of the Alemannic dukes, looking over from the castle onto the "Hohentwiel". The self-confidence of the citizenry only developed when Konstanz became a free Imperial city.

Dann das Jahr 1414: Mit ihm kommen Delegierte aus dem gesamten Abendland, Patriarchen, Kardinäle, Erzbischöfe, geistliche Fürsten, jeweils mit Gefolge, dazu Anwälte, Sekretäre, Doctores und Priester – aber auch Händler, Huren und Ganoven. 60.000 bis 70.000 Fremde sollen sich in Konstanz aufgehalten haben. Der Grund: Das erste und einzige Konzil auf deutschem Boden, bei dem Otto von Colonna, genannt Martin V., 1418 zum Papst gewählt wurde.

Then the year 1414: with it came delegates from all over the western world, patriarchs, cardinals, archbishops, princes of the Church, each with their retinue, together with procurators, secretaries, doctors and priests – and also merchants, prostitutes and villains. 60,000 to 70,000 people are supposed to have stayed in Konstanz. The reason: the first and only Council on German soil, at which Otto von Colonna was elected Pope Martin V in 1418.

Die vielen Fremden in der Stadt wollten versorgt werden. Die Fischer schafften es kaum, genügend Fisch aus dem See zu ziehen; Nachschub aus Italien musste her. Bier war unüblich, und so brachten sich die Bischöfe von Oppeln und Breslau je ein Fass Bier aus der Heimat mit. Der Minnesänger Oswald von Wolkenstein reimt später: „Denk' ich an den Bodensee, tut mir gleich der Beutel weh!"

The many strangers in the town needed to be fed. The fishermen could hardly manage to haul enough fish out of the lake, and extra provisions had to be brought in from Italy. Beer was unusual, and so the Bishops of Oppeln and Breslau each brought with them a barrel of beer from home. The minstrel Oswald von Wolkenstein later rhymed: "Denk' ich an den Bodensee, tut mir gleich der Beutel weh!" ("Whenever I think of the Bodensee, I recall how much I had to pay").

Die Aufgabe des Konzils war es, die Kirchenspaltung mitsamt ihren drei Päpsten zur selben Zeit zu beenden und strittige Glaubensfragen zu lösen. Deshalb wurde auch der gebannte Reformator Jan Hus nach Konstanz geladen. König Sigismund sicherte ihm freies Geleit zu. Hus kam, seine Exkommunikation wurde aufgehoben, doch kurz darauf wurde er unter einem Vorwand festgenommen, angeklagt und als Ketzer verbrannt. Dasselbe Schicksal widerfuhr dem Reformator Hieronymus von Prag.

The task of the Council was to bring an end to the schism of the Church, with its three popes, and at the same time resolve disputed questions of faith. The excommunicated reformer Jan Hus was therefore also...

invited to Konstanz. King Sigismund guaranteed him safe conduct. Hus came, and his excommunication was lifted, but shortly after he was arrested on a pretext, tried and burnt for heresy. The same fate befell the reformer Hieronymus of Prague.

Danach schlossen sich die Würdenträger drei Tage und Nächte lang zur Papstwahl im alten Kaufhaus am Hafen ein, das deshalb heute „Konzil" genannt wird. Nach erfolgreicher Wahl reiste der Tross ab. Sigismund, der mit Königin Barbara und Gefolge jahrelang in Konstanz gelebt hatte, prellte den größten Teil seiner Zeche. *The dignitaries then shut themselves away for three days and nights in the old store by the harbour for the papal election, which is therefore called the "Council" today. Following the successful conclusion of the election, the assembly departed. Sigismund, who had lived in Konstanz for years with Queen Barbara and their retinue, left with most of their bills unpaid.*

Bauernschläue bewiesen die Konstanzer im Zweiten Weltkrieg. Als die Bombengeschwader über den See flogen, taten es die Konstanzer der neutralen Nachbarstadt Kreuzlingen gleich. In Deutschland herrschte Verdunklungsgebot. Doch die Konstanzer ließen ihre Lichter an. So konnten die Flieger nicht unterscheiden, ob dies nun neutrales oder feindliches Gebiet war, und Konstanz blieb von Zerstörungen verschont. *In the Second World War, the people of Konstanz demonstrated their cunning. When the bombers flew over the lake, they did the same as the neutral, neighbouring town of Kreuzlingen. In Germany there was a blackout. But the people of Konstanz left their lights on, so that the flyers could not tell whether this was neutral or enemy territory, and Konstanz remained spared from destruction.*

Bischof Radolf errichtete im 9. Jahrhundert eine Zelle am westlichen Rand des Sees: Radolfzell. Heute ist Radolfzell eine Kleinstadt mit schönen Gassen und malerischen Nischen und einem österreichischen Schlösschen. Das erinnert daran, dass Radolfzell von 1298 bis 1806, von einem Intermezzo als freie Reichsstadt abgesehen, zu Österreich gehörte. Im Mittelalter zog es Pilger von weither zu den Reliquien der Märtyrer Senesius und Theopont sowie den Gebeinen des Veroneser Bischofs Zeno. Heute kommen Erholungssuchende und Kurgäste. Im Juli feiern die Radolfzeller mit einer Prozession das Hausherrenfest zu Ehren ihrer Schutzheiligen. Dazu gehört auch die Mooser Wasserprozession. Dann schickt die Nachbargemeinde Moos blumengeschmückte Boote über den See aus Dankbarkeit, dass ihr Vieh 1796 durch den Beistand der „Hausherren" von der grassierenden Viehseuche verschont blieb. *In the 9th Century, Bishop Radolf built a cell on the western edge of the lake: Radolfzell. Today Radolfzell is a small town of quaint alleyways and picturesque niches, and a small Austrian castle. This recalls the fact that apart from a brief spell as a free imperial city, Radolfzell belonged to Austria from 1298 to 1806. In the Middle Ages, it drew pilgrims from far and wide to see the relics of the martyrs Senesius and Theopont and the bones of the Veronese Bishop Zeno. Today it attracts those seeking rest, relaxation and recuperation. In July, the people of Radolfzell organise a procession in celebration of the "Hausherrenfest" in honour of their patron saints. This also includes the Moos "Wasserprozession" ("Water procession") when the neighbouring community of Moos sends flower-bedecked boats onto the lake in gratitude for the assistance of the "Hausherren" in sparing their cattle from the rampant cattle plague of 1796.*

„Jetzt hör i auf", soll Gott gesagt, sich die Lehmreste von den Fingern gestreift und zufrieden auf sein letztes Werk geschaut haben: eine hügelig bewaldete, fruchtbare Halbinsel – die Höri. „Jetzt hör i auf." In den Höri-Dörfern ließen sich Maler und Schriftsteller nieder, beschaulich geht es heute zu im „Gottesgarten am See". *"Jetzt hör i auf" ("Now I have finished"), God is supposed to have said, wiping the*

remains of clay from his hands and looking down with satisfaction on his last work: a hilly, wooded, fertile peninsula – the Höri. "Jetzt hör i auf:" Painters and authors settled here in the Höri villages, and life today is placid here in "God's garden on the lake".

Seit dem Dreißigjährigen Krieg siedelten sich Juden auf der Höri an, Gailingen war sogar die größte jüdische Landgemeinde Deutschlands. Doch die Pogrome der Nazis griffen auch auf die Höri über, und 1940 wurden die letzten verbliebenen 200 Gailinger Juden deportiert. *Jews settled on the Höri since the Thirty Years War, and Gailingen became the largest Jewish rural community in Germany. But the pogroms of the Nazis also extended to the Höri, and in 1940 the last remaining 200 Jews of Gailingen were deported.*

Prächtige Stadttore, bunt bemalte Bürgerhäuser in engen Gassen, geteilt durch den Rhein schmiegt sich Stein am Rhein mit seinen pittoresken Häuschen, den spitzen Türmen und auskragenden Erkern an den Fluss. Stein am Rhein erlaubt fast einen direkten Blick zurück ins 13. Jahrhundert. Schon damals war das Städtchen von Mauern umschlossen, schon damals ging es geschäftig zu. Denn hier wurden die Waren zum Weitertransport nach Schaffhausen auf kleinere Schiffe umgeladen. Ein Warenumschlagplatz, aber auch Lager- und Handelsstadt. *Magnificent town gates, brightly painted merchants' houses lining narrow alleyways, divided by the Rhein, Stein am Rhein with its picturesque little houses, pointed spires and projecting alcoves huddles around the river. Stein am Rhein allows an almost direct look back into the 13th Century. Even then the town was enclosed by walls, even then it was a bustling centre, where goods were offloaded and transferred to smaller ships for onward transport to Schaffhausen. A centre of transhipment, storage of goods and brisk trade.*

Von Stein am Rhein ist es nicht weit zum Rheinfall, dessen mächtige Stromschnellen schon immer die Handelswege unterbrochen haben. Auf einer Breite von mehr als 150 Meter stürzt sich der Rhein 25 Meter in die Tiefe. Es spritzt, brodelt, donnert, schäumt, tost und gluckst. Gischtnebel. Regenbogen auf den tanzenden Wellen. Der Dichter Johann Wolfgang von Goethe hielt sich 1797 einen ganzen Tag am größten Wasserfall Europas auf, um sich dem „Naturphänomen in seinem vollen Glanze" zu widmen. „Wenn die strömenden Stellen grün aussehen, so erscheint der nächste Gischt leise purpur gefärbt." Sein Kollege Eduard Mörike sah mit zitterndem Herzen „donnernde Massen auf donnernde Massen geworfen. Ohr und Auge wohin retten sie sich im Tumult?" *From Stein am Rhein, it is not far to the Rhein Falls, whose powerful rapids have always been a hindrance to the trade routes. At a width of over 150 metres, the Rhein crashes 25 metres into the depths. It splashes, seethes, thunders, foams, rages and gurgles. A mist of spray, with a rainbow above the dancing waves. The poet Johann Wolfgang von Goethe stopped here at the greatest waterfall in Europe for a whole day in 1797, in order to devote himself to the "natural phenomenon in its full glory." "When the flowing waters look green, the next spray appears with a slight purple tinge." His colleague Eduard Mörike, with trembling heart, saw "thundering masses cast on thundering masses, no refuge for the ears or eyes in this tumult?"*

Am Untersee gefiel es schon vor Jahrhunderten den Leuten mit ein bisschen mehr Geld. Kaufleute errichteten ihre Landsitze, und auch der Hochadel ließ sich hier nieder. So herrscht am Untersee eine hohe Dichte an Schlössern und Villen. Gottlieben, Triboltingen, Berlingen, Mammern, Steckborn, Eschenz – kaum ein Dorf, das nicht damit aufwarten kann. Allen voran Schloss Arenenberg, das über den Weinbergen von Salenstein thront und zum Exil für Angehörige des verbannten Napoleons wurde.

Von 1830 bis 1837 lebte Hortense de Beauharnais hier, Frankreichs ausgewiesene Königin und Napoleons I. Stieftochter. Ihr Sohn Louis, der spätere Kaiser Napoleon III., wuchs im Schloss auf und wurde 1832 Ehrenbürger. Seinetwegen wäre es 1838 beinahe zum Krieg zwischen Frankreich und der Schweiz gekommen, weil diese ihn Ehrenbürger nicht ausliefern wollte. Schließlich verließ er freiwillig den Thurgau in Richtung England. *Centuries ago, the Untersee was discovered by people with a little more money. Rich merchants built their country estates here, and the high nobility also settled here. The Untersee is surrounded by dozens of castles and villas. Gottlieben, Triboltingen, Berlingen, Mammern, Steckborn, Eschenz – hardly a single village which does not boast one of them. And above all "Schloss Arenenberg", which sits enthroned above the vineyards of Salenstein, and became the place of exile for followers of the banished Napoleon. From 1830 to 1837 it was the home of Hortense de Beauharnais, France's banished queen and stepdaughter of Napoleon I. Her son Louis, later to become Emperor Napoleon III, grew up in the castle, and became an honorary citizen in 1832. It was on his account that it almost came to war between France and Switzerland in 1838, when the latter refused to give up its honorary citizen. He finally left Thurgau voluntarily, heading for England.*

Schon während des Konstanzer Konzils bekam der Fischerort Ermatingen die „Groppenfasnacht". Als der Gegenpapst Johannes XXIII., einer der drei Männer, die damals gleichzeitig den Stuhl Petri für sich beanspruchten, fluchtartig Konstanz verließ, kam er unerkannt nach Ermatingen, so die Legende. Die Ermatinger nahmen den Fremden freundlich auf und versorgten ihn mit Groppen. Das sind kleine Fische, die am Ufer unter Steinen leben und geräuchert werden. Der Papst, formell noch in Amt und Würden, verfügte angeblich, dass den freundlichen Ermatingern für alle Zeit eine verlängerte Fastnacht gestattet sei, die nun alle drei Jahre stattfindet. Dort am Untersee, wo die Landschaft lieblich ist, überschaubar. *During the Council of Constance, the fishing village of Ermatingen was endowed with the "Groppenfasnacht" ("Bullhead Carnival"). When the antipope Johannes XXIII, one of the three men claiming the throne of St. Peter at the time, hastily left Konstanz, he arrived unrecognised in Ermatingen, so the legend goes. The people of Ermatingen received the stranger with kindness, and provided him with bullheads. These are small fish which live under stones close to the bank, and are caught and smoked. The Pope, officially still in office, ordained that the friendly people of Ermatingen could in perpetuity enjoy an extended Carnival which now takes place every three years. Here on the Untersee, where the landscape is cosy and more manageable.*

REICHENAU: RETTICH UND ROMANTIK *RADISHES AND ROMANTICISM*

Rings von Wassern wild umbrandet,
Stehst du fest, ein Fels der Liebe,
Streust weit und breit der Lehre
Samenkörner, sel'ge Insel.
(Walahfrid Strabo)

Surrounded by raging waters
You stand fast, a rock of love
Spreading far and wide the teaching
Bounteous seeds, blessed Isle.
(Walahfrid Strabo)

Sel'ge Insel Reichenau. Reiche Au. Eine lange Pappelallee, rechts und links Schilf, dann Wasser. Erst seit 1838 kann man trockenen Fußes auf die Insel gelangen, seit der Damm aufgeschüttet und die Pappelallee gepflanzt worden ist. Zuvor gab es lediglich eine Furt, die man nur bei niedrigem Wasserstand passieren konnte. *The blessed isle of Reichenau. "Reiche Au" ("rich pasture"). A long avenue of poplars, reeds to the right and left, and then water. Only since 1838 has it been possible to reach the island with dry*

feet, since the construction of the embankment and the planting of the poplars. Before this time there was only a ford, which could only be passed at low water.

Salatbeet reiht sich an Salatbeet, dazu Brokkoli, Lauch, Tomaten, Gurken, Spinat und Rettiche. Die Reichenau ist eine Gemüseinsel. 2,4 Quadratkilometer, mehr als die Hälfte der Inselfläche, dienen dem Gemüseanbau, davon ein halber Quadratkilometer in Gewächshäusern. Nicht der Salatköpfe wegen, sondern wegen ihrer Vergangenheit als kulturelle, politische, künstlerische und geistliche Keimzelle Mitteleuropas und ihrer alten Mönchskultur zählt die Reichenau seit 2001 zum UNESCO-Weltkulturerbe. Seit mehr als eintausend Jahren gehen Natur und Kultur hier eine harmonische Verbindung ein.

Rows upon rows of beet, together with broccoli, leeks, tomatoes, cucumbers, spinach and radishes. Reichenau is an island of vegetables. 2.4 km², more than half the area of the island, is devoted to vegetable-growing, including half a square kilometre of greenhouses. Reichenau has been a UNESCO world cultural heritage site since 2001, not because of its vegetables, but because of its history as a cultural, political, artistic and spiritual nucleus of central Europe and its old monastic culture. Nature and culture have been in harmony here for more than 1,000 years.

Als sich der Wandermönch Pirmin 724 auf das Eiland übersetzen ließ, soll die größte Bodenseeinsel eine unwirtliche gewesen sein. Es hauste dort, so will es die Sage, „giftiges Gewürm": Schlangen und Kröten. Als Pirmin allerdings seinen Fuß auf die Reichenau setzte, floh das Getier und stürzte sich in

Mit Walahfrid Strabo lebt auf der Reichenau einer der bedeutendsten Dichter des Mittelalters. Sein wohl populärstes Werk ist „Liber de cultura hortorum", das „Buch über den Gartenbau". Darin beschreibt er 24 Pflanzen, die im Klostergarten wachsen, deren Heilkräfte, aber auch was es an Arbeit im Garten zu tun gibt, damit nicht das Unkraut den Boden überwuchert, die Pflanzen nicht vor Durst erschlaffen. *In Walahfrid Strabo, Reichenau was home to one of the most important writers of the Middle Ages. Probably his most popular work is the "Liber de cultura hortorum", the "book on market gardening". Here he described 24 plants which grew in the monastery garden, their healing powers, and all the work to be done in the garden, so that the soil would not become infested with weeds, or the plants wither from lack of water.*

Im 11. Jahrhundert gilt Abt Hermann der Lahme, körperlich schwerstbehindert, als einer der klügsten Köpfe seiner Zeit. Doch im Laufe der Zeit geht die Zahl der Mönche zurück, zudem brennt 1238 das Kloster und verarmt. Mitte des 18. Jahrhunderts wird es endgültig aufgelöst. *In the 11th Century, Abbot Hermann the Lame, although physically severely handicapped, was considered to be one of the cleverest minds of his time. But over the course of time, the number of monks declined, the monastery burnt down in 1238 and became impoverished, and it was finally given up in the mid-18th Century.*

Seit 2004 versuchen zwei Benediktinermönche an die uralten klösterlichen Traditionen anzuknüpfen. Sie haben eine „Cella St. Benedikt" gegründet, die der Erzabtei Beuron im Kreis Sigmaringen zugeordnet ist. Insgesamt leben heute etwa 3.500 Menschen, meist Landwirte, Winzer und Fischer, auf der Reichenau. *Since 2004, two Benedictine monks have been trying to revive the ancient monastic traditions. They have founded a "Cella St. Benedikt", which comes under the Archabbey of Beuron in the Sigmaringen district. Today about 3.500 people live on Reichenau, mainly farmers, vintners and fishermen.*

Von der kunsthistorischen Bedeutung des Klosters zeugen die ottonischen Wandmalereien, die im 10. Jahrhundert in der Stiftskirche St. Georg in Oberzell gemalt wurden und die Wundertaten Jesu zeigen. Kunsthistorisch wichtig ist auch das restaurierte Marienmünster in Mittelzell mit seinem offenen Dachstuhl. Wertvolle Wandgemälde wurden erst im Jahr 1900 in der Kirche St. Peter und Paul entdeckt. *The art history importance of the monastery is indicated by the Ottonian wall paintings which were painted in the 10th Century in the monastery church of St. Georg in Oberzell, and which depict the miracles performed by Jesus. Equally important in art history is the restored "Marienmünster" in Mittelzell with its open roof truss. Valuable wall paintings in the church of St. Peter and Paul were only discovered in the year 1900.*

Bis heute hat sich die Reichenau ihre besondere Aura von Ruhe trotz aller Betriebsamkeit bewahren können. *Despite the bustle of modern life, Reichenau has been able to preserve its special aura of calm to the present day.*

Reichenau, grünendes Eiland, wie bist du vor anderen gesegnet,
Reich an Schätzen des Wissens und heiligem Sinn der Bewohner,
Reich an des Obstbaums Frucht und schwellender Traube des Weinbergs;
Immerdar blüht es auf dir und spiegelt im See sich die Lilie,
Weithin schallet dein Ruhm bis ins neblige Land der Britannen.
(Emmerich von Ellwangen, um 850)

den See. *When the itinerant monk Pirmin had himself carried to the island in 724, this largest island in Lake Constance was not said to be quite so hospitable. It was said to be the home of "poisonous serpents": snakes and toads. But when Pirmin set foot on Reichenau, the vermin fled and threw themselves into the lake.*

Pirmin wird der erste Abt der „richen auwe" und legt den Grundstein für den Ausbau zur Klosterinsel mit 20 Kirchen und Kapellen. Abt Walahfrid gründet im 9. Jahrhundert eine Gelehrtenschule samt Bibliothek, mit 400 Büchern ist sie die umfangreichste des Abendlandes. Die Sammlung ist immens, werden Bücher doch damals noch aufwändig von Hand geschrieben und vervielfältigt.

Die Reichenau wird zur „Schule der Nation", zur Kaderschmiede der Karolinger. Denn Karl der Große mit seinem Riesenreich benötigt gut ausgebildete, schreib- und lesekundige Verwalter für seinen ausgedehnten Besitz. *Pirmin became the first Abbot of the "richen auwe" ("rich pasture") and laid the foundations for the development into a monastic island with 20 churches and chapels.*

In the 9th Century, Abbot Walahfrid founded a grammar school and library, which with a collection of 400 books was the most comprehensive in the western world. The collection was huge for the time, since books were still painstakingly written and copied by hand. Reichenau became the "school of the nation", the elite training centre of the Carolingians, because Charlemagne with his huge empire needed well-educated people who could read and write for the administration of his extensive possessions.

Reichenau, verdant island, how you are blessed above others,
Rich in treasures of knowledge and piety of its people,
Rich in the bounty of fruit and swelling grapes of the vineyard;
Always in blossom, the lilies reflected by the lake,
Your fame rings out far to the misty land of the Britons.
(Emmerich von Ellwangen, around 850)

MALER, SCHRIFTSTELLER UND SCHMUGGLER PAINTERS, AUTHORS AND SMUGGLERS

„Das einzige Komfortable im Hause war ein schöner alter Kachelofen (...). Wasser gab es im Hause nicht, das musste vom Brunnen in der Nähe geholt werden, Gas oder elektrisches Licht gab es in der ganzen Gegend nicht, und es war auch nicht ganz einfach, das Dörfchen zu erreichen oder zu verlassen (...). Es war aber gerade das, was wir uns gewünscht hatten, ein verwunschenes, verborgenes Nest ohne Lärm, mit reiner Luft, mit See und Wald", so beschrieb Hermann Hesse sein neues Zuhause, als er sich 1904 in Gaienhofen niederließ. Mit ihm begann die Künstler-Ära auf der Höri. Frisch verheiratet lebte Hesse in dem 300-Seelen-Dorf und schrieb in einem Brief an Alexander Freiherr von Bernus: „Unser Leben hier ist völlig einsam und ländlich, doch nicht ganz, was man poetisch-idyllisch nennt. Das Dörflein ist ganz klein und hat nur einen Bäcker, aber keine Läden, keinen Metzger. Ich muss also nach Steckborn rudern und dort einkaufen. Dabei wird der Zoll passiert, und ich kann schon den ganzen Zolltarif für Küchensachen auswendig, ziehe aber natürlich wo möglich das Schmuggeln vor." Acht Jahre lebte Hesse auf der Höri. „Dieses südwestdeutsch-schweizerische Gebiet ist mir Heimat", schrieb er. *"The only comfort in the house was a beautiful old tiled stove (...), there was no water to the house, that had to be fetched from the nearby well, there was no gas or electric light in the whole region, and it was also not very easy to reach or to leave the village (...). It was nevertheless exactly what we had wanted, an enchanted, hidden nest without noise, with clean air, lake and forest", this was how Hermann Hesse described his new home when he settled in Gaienhofen in 1904. With him began the artists' era on the Höri. Recently married, Hesse lived in this village of 300 souls, and wrote in a letter to Alexander Freiherr von Bernus: "Our life here is completely secluded and rural, although not quite what one might call poetically idyllic. The village is very small and has only one baker, but no shops, no butcher, so I have to row to Steckborn for my shopping, I have to pass the customs post, and I already know by heart all the customs duties for provisions, although I naturally prefer smuggling whenever possible." Hesse lived on the Höri for eight years. "This southwest German-Swiss region is home to me", he wrote.*

Die Gegend wurde bald zum Anziehungspunkt für Schriftsteller wie Ludwig Finck oder Hans Leip. Auch Werner Dürrson lebte in den siebziger und achtziger Jahren im Höridorf Kattenhorn. In seinem „Kattenhorner Schweigen" thematisiert er sarkastisch und gewitzt die Verbauung am See. *The region soon attracted other writers such as Ludwig Finck and Hans Leip. Werner Dürrson also lived in the Höri village of Kattenhorn in the 70s and 80s. In his "Kattenhorner Schweigen", he sarcastically and cunningly criticises the development being carried out around the lake.*

Die Maler Otto Dix, Erich Heckel, Helmut Macke und Max Ackermann kamen auf die Höri und malten sie. Einige von ihnen waren nicht freiwillig an den Untersee gekommen. Otto Dix etwa ist auf der Höri in die innere Emigration gegangen, nachdem er 1933 von den Nationalsozialisten als Professor an der Dresdner Kunstakademie abgesetzt worden war. Die freie Schweiz war zum Greifen nah und doch unerreichbar. Max Ackermann, damals schon ein abstrakter Maler, hatte immer ein angefangenes, dem Regime vorzeigbares Bild in seinem Atelier, um bei überraschenden Kontrollbesuchen Harmlosigkeit demonstrieren zu können. *The painters Otto Dix, Erich Heckel, Helmut Macke and Max Ackermann all came to the Höri and painted it. Some of them were not on the Untersee by choice. Otto Dix for example was sent to the Höri in internal exile, after he was dismissed from his post as Professor at the Dresden Academy of Art by the National Socialists in 1933. Free Switzerland was close enough to touch, but still unreachable. Max Ackermann, already an abstract painter at the time, always had a started painting in his studio which was acceptable to the regime, in order to be able to demonstrate his harmlessness in case of unexpected inspection visits.*

Nicht auf der Höri, sondern auf der Schweizer Seite des Untersees, in Berlingen, lebte von 1877 bis 1957 der Waldarbeiter, Tagelöhner und Maler Adolf Dietrich. Hemdsärmelig, zupackend, aber auch genau beobachtend. Schon früh hielt der Autodidakt im Stile alter Meister seinen ländlichen Kosmos in Öl fest. Bekannt gemacht haben ihn seine im naiven Stil, doch mit beinahe wissenschaftlicher Präzision gemalten Bilder von Tieren, Landschaften und Bauerngärten. Seine Bilder wurden in London, New York, Paris und Berlin gezeigt, doch Dietrich war und blieb in Berlingen und gab sein einfaches Leben nicht auf. *From 1877 to 1957, the woodsman, labourer and painter Adolf Dietrich lived not on the Höri, but on the Swiss side of the Untersee, in Berlingen. Down-to-earth, hard-working, but also very observant. In his early years, this self-taught painter captured his rural surroundings in oil in the style of the old masters. He became known for his pictures of animals, landscapes and cottage gardens painted in the naïve style, yet with almost scientific precision. His pictures were exhibited in London, New York, Paris and Berlin, although Dietrich remained in Berlingen and stuck to his simple life.*

EIN LAUSCHIGES PLÄTZCHEN IM SCHILF A SECLUDED SPOT AMONGST THE REEDS

Im Wollmatinger Ried und auf der Halbinsel Mettnau herrschen ein Kommen und Gehen. Fast eine Million Vögel aus dem hohen Norden und aus Osteuropa überwintern am Bodensee. Im Naturschutzgebiet Wollmatinger Ried wurde ein Rastplatz für Wasservögel geschaffen. Das Schilf und die Riedwiesen bieten Schutz und Lebensraum. Für den seltenen Singschwan zum Beispiel, der ruhig, fast mit Anmut sein Gefieder putzt. Die Singschwäne finden sich im Dezember ein, meist als letzte der hier überwinternden Vogelarten, denn sie haben die weiteste Anreise. Viele von ihnen kommen bis vom Polarkreis. Zu Dutzenden treffen sich dann Ornithologen am Untersee, um die Singschwäne zu beobachten. Die Flachwasserzonen des Rieds sind nicht nur Rastplatz, sondern auch Brut-, Nahrungs-, Aufzucht- und Ruheplatz etwa für Eisvögel, Knäkenten, Haubentaucher, Löffelenten, Graureiher, Schwarzhalsstorche und die seltenen Kolbenenten. *There is always much coming and going in the Wollmatinger Ried and on the Mettnau peninsula. Almost one million birds from the far north and eastern Europe winter on Lake Constance. A resting place for waterfowl has been created in the nature conservation area of the Wollmatinger Ried. The reeds and reed meadows offer protection and habitat. For example for the rare whooper swan, which cleans its plumage calmly, almost with grace. The whooper swans arrive in December, usually as the last species to winter here, because they have the longest journey. Many of them come from the Arctic Circle. Ornithologists then come to the Untersee by the dozen to observe them. The calm water areas of the Ried are not only a resting place, but also a breeding, feeding and rearing place for species such as kingfishers, garganey ducks, great crested grebe, shoveller ducks, grey herons, black-necked storks and the rare red-crested pochards.*

Genauso ist es bei der Vogelwarte Radolfzell auf der Halbinsel Mettnau. Dort werden die Vögel beringt, damit ihr Zugverhalten erforscht werden kann. Beinahe stündlich suchen Praktikanten, Studenten oder Ehrenamtliche die Netze im Schilf nach Vögeln ab. Vorsichtig werden die Vögel aus den Netzen geholt, vermessen, bestimmt und mit einem Ring versehen. So kann die Reise der Zugvögel erforscht werden, die auch für die Menschen von Bedeutung ist, nicht erst, seit es Krankheiten wie die Vogelgrippe gibt. *The same applies to the Radolfzell Ornithological Station on the Mettnau peninsula. Here the birds are ringed in order to determine their migration patterns. Almost every hour, trainees,*

students or volunteers check the nets in the reeds for birds. The birds are carefully retrieved from the nets, checked, measured and ringed. In this way, their migratory habits can be researched, which is also important for people, particularly since the development of such diseases as avian flu.

Doch wenn über den Schilfhälsen nur die weißen Dreiecke der Segel zu sehen sind, das Plätschern der Wellen und das Zwitschern der Vögel zu hören ist, dann denkt niemand an Krankheiten, sondern lässt sich ganz von der friedlichen Atmosphäre einnehmen. *But when only the white triangles of the sails can be seen above the reeds, when the splashing of the waves and the twittering of the birds can be heard, nobody thinks of diseases, giving themselves up instead to the peaceful atmosphere.*

Geprägt ist das 767 Hektar große Naturreservat, das größte am Bodensee, von den unterschiedlichen Wasserständen des Sees. Durch die Schneeschmelze in den Alpen wird es vom späten Frühjahr an überflutet. Dadurch entwickelt sich eine vielfältige Vegetation. Von mehr als 600 im Wollmatinger Ried festgestellten Pflanzenarten stehen mehr als 100 auf der Roten Liste des Landes Baden-Württemberg. Blaues Pfeifengras, Lungen-Enzian, Sumpf-Siegwurz, Sibirische Schwertlilie, Bienen-Ragwurz und Sumpf-Gladiole kommen im Ried vor. Die Sumpf-Gladiole ist nur noch hier bekannt. Im Ried tummeln sich auch 330 Schmetterlings- und 50 Libellenarten. Schilf wiegt sich im Wind, Enten quaken, Vögel

zwitschern, Libellen summen. Damit sich Flora und Fauna nahezu ungestört entfalten können, ist das Wollmatinger Ried für den Menschen nur bei Riedführungen zugänglich. *The 1,900-acre nature reserve, the largest on Lake Constance, is characterised by the different water levels of the lake. From late spring, it is flooded by meltwater from the Alps. This gives rise to its varied vegetation. Of over 600 plant species identified in the Wollmatinger Ried, more than 100 are on the danger list of the state of Baden-Württemberg. Purple moor grass, autumn gentian, swamp gladiola, Siberian lily and bee orchid all occur in the Ried. The swamp gladiola is found nowhere else. The Ried is also home to 330 species of butterflies and 50 species of dragonflies. The reeds sway in the wind, ducks quack, birds twitter, dragonflies buzz. So that the flora and fauna can live almost undisturbed, the Wollmatinger Ried can only be seen by people on guided tours.*

Schon Anfang des 15. Jahrhunderts erlangte Konstanz internationale Bedeutung, weil während des „Konstanzer Konzils" die einzige je nördlich der Alpen durchgeführte Papstwahl stattfand. Heute ist die an der Schweizer Grenze gelegene Universitätsstadt die größte Stadt am Bodensee und ein Anziehungspunkt für Wassersportler.

As early as the beginning of the 15th Century, Konstanz attained international importance, because during the "Council of Constance", the only papal election to be held north of the Alps, took place here. Today, this university city located on the Swiss border is the largest city on Lake Constance and a centre of attraction for water sports enthusiasts.

Konstanz liegt am Ausfluss des Rheins aus dem Obersee. Mehrere Brücken überqueren den Fluss und verbinden die Konstanzer Altstadt mit den neueren Stadtteilen auf dem Bodanrück. Im Hintergrund sind der beleuchtete Rheintorturm und das Münster zu sehen.

Konstanz lies on the "Obersee" at the outlet of the Rhein. Several bridges span the river connecting the old town of Konstanz with the more modern parts of the city on the "Bodanrück". The illuminated "Rheintorturm" and the Münster can be seen in the background.

Schemenhaft breitet Peter Lenks „Imperia" an der Konstanzer Hafeneinfahrt ihre Arme im herbstlichen Nebel aus. Die während des Sommers so belebte Hafenmole erscheint jetzt wie ausgestorben.

Her outline blurred by the autumn mist, Peter Lenk's "Imperia" holds up her arms at the Konstanz harbour entrance. The harbour mole so busy in summer now looks abandoned and deserted.

Wer die Gemüseinsel Reichenau besucht, wird bei Oberzell von einer Steinfigur des Schutzpatrons Sankt Pirmin empfangen. Die im Jahre 2000 ins UNESCO-Weltkulturerbe aufgenommene Insel ist von kleinen Wanderwegen durchzogen. Inmitten der Felder Niederzells erhebt sich die im 11. Jahrhundert erbaute romanische Säulenbasilika St. Peter und Paul.

Anyone visiting the vegetable island of Reichenau will be received at Oberzell by a stone statue of the patron St. Pirmin. Designated a UNESCO world cultural heritage site in the year 2000, the island is criss-crossed by short footpaths. In the middle of the fields of Niederzell rises the 11th Century Roman basilica of St. Peter and Paul.

Vom Höhrenberg aus bietet sich ein fantastischer Blick über das Städtchen Allensbach, den Gnadensee und die Insel Reichenau bis zum Schiener Berg und in den Hegau hinein.

The "Höhrenberg" offers a breathtaking view of the small town of Allensbach, the Gnadensee and the island of Reichenau, and on to the "Schiener Berg" and the Hegau

Ein großer Teil der Halbinsel Mettnau ist als Naturschutzgebiet ausgewiesen und darf nicht betreten werden. Die Feldstation der Vogelwarte Radolfzell hat hier an die 270 Vogelarten gezählt.

A large part of the Mettnau peninsula is a designated nature preservation area, and is out of bounds to the public. The field station of the Radolfzell Ornithological Station has identified around 270 species of birds here, either resident or on passage.

74

An der Hafenmole Radolfzells hat der Landschaftskünstler Sepp Bögle seine Steinskulpturen errichtet. In den Sommermonaten hält der Künstler dort Hof und plaudert mit Einheimischen und Besuchern über seine Lebensphilosophie, seine Kunst und vieles andere.

The landscape artist Sepp Bögle created his stone sculptures here by the harbour mole at Radolfzell. In the summer months, the artist holds court here, and chats with locals and visitors about his philosophy of life, his art and many other subjects.

Einer Märchenlandschaft gleicht das Radolfzeller Ried im Morgennebel. Die Sonne, die über dem Bodanrück aufgeht, wird die Nebelschwa-
den bald vertreiben.

The fairytale landscape of the "Radolfzeller Ried" rises out of the morning mist, which will soon be evaporated by the sun rising over the "Bodanrück".

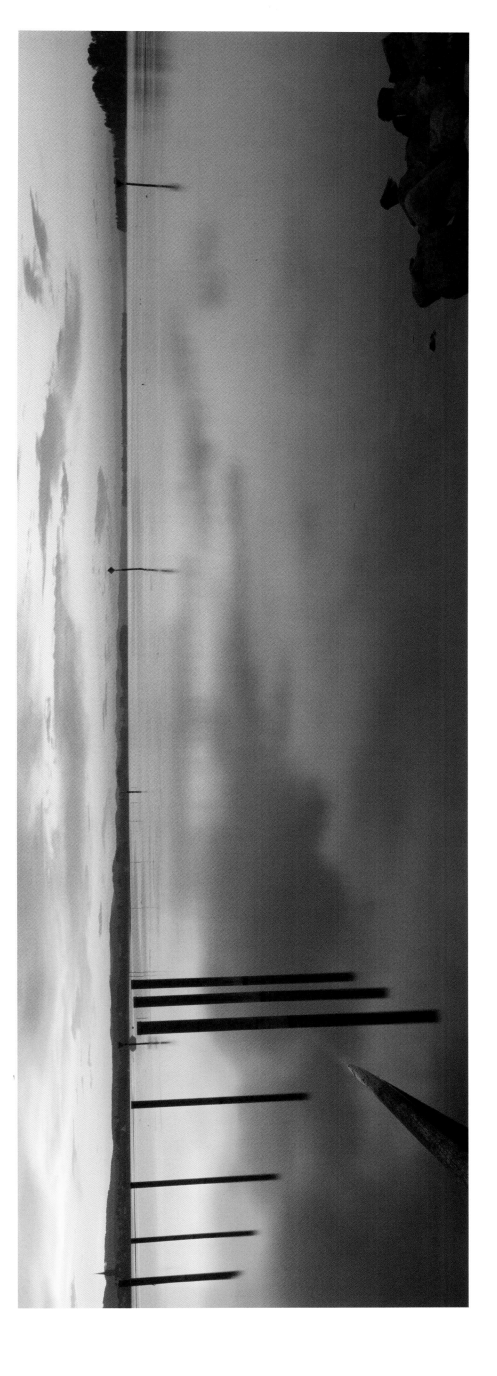

Moos. Red sky in the morning over the "Zeller See".

Moos. Morgenröte über dem Zeller See.

Herbstnebel zwischen Moos und Iznang. Der schwere Moorboden dieser Gegend eignet sich besonders gut zum Anbau von Zwiebeln, die man hier „Bülle" nennt.

Autumn mist between Moos and Iznang. The heavy, peaty soil of this region is particularly good for growing onions, which the local people call "Bülle".

Wie jeder der kleinen Uferorte auf der Halbinsel Höri hat auch Iznang seine eigene Schiffslandestelle und seinen Hafen.

Like all the villages along the shore of the Höri peninsula, Iznang has its own landing stage and harbour.

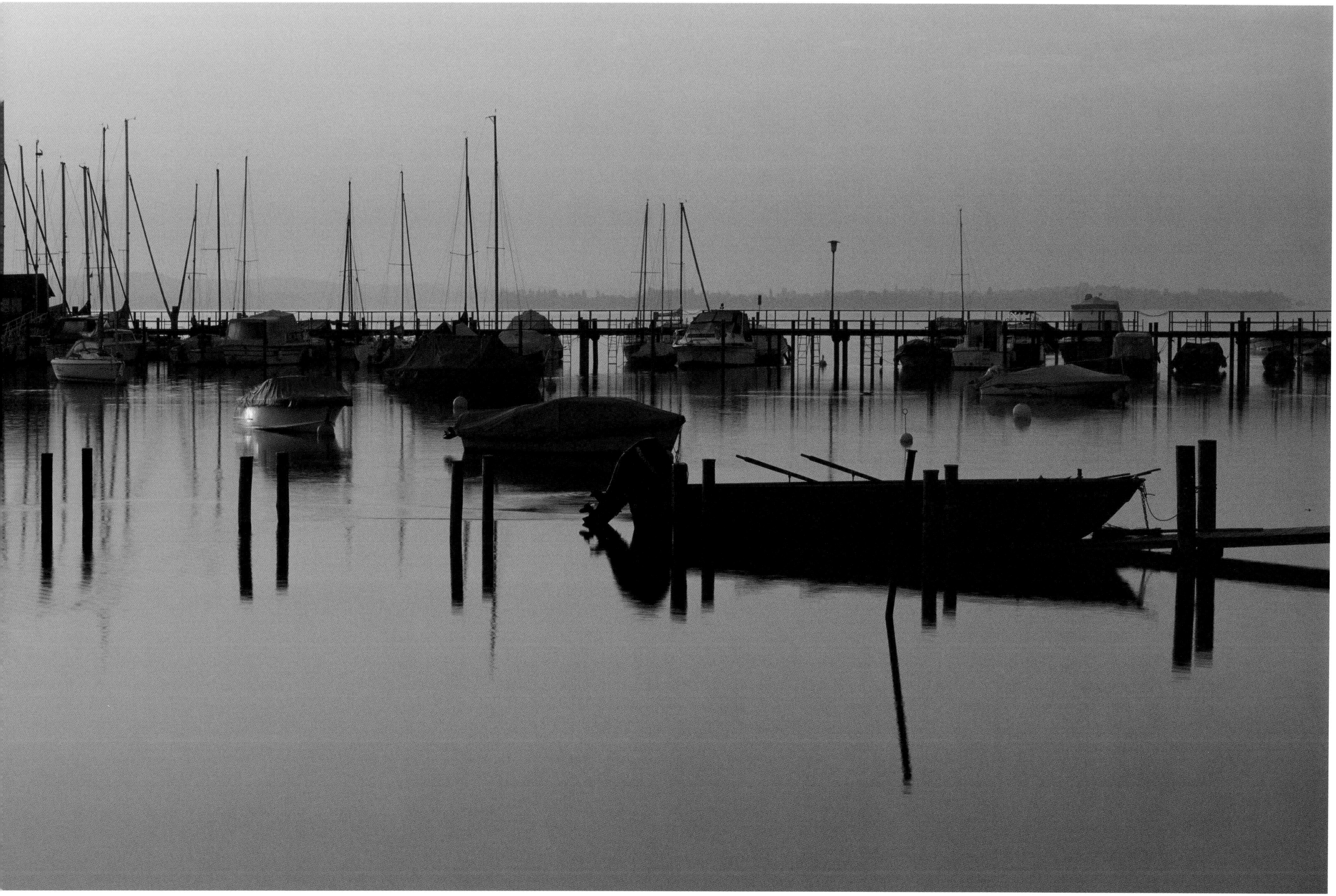

Die Pfarrkirche der kleinen Gemeinde Horn liegt auf einem steil abfallenden Hang mit herrlichem Blick über den Untersee und die wind-zerzauste Uferlandschaft.

The Parish Church of the small community of Horn stands on a steeply descending slope with a magnificent view over the Untersee and the windswept shore landscape.

Noch träumt das Horner Ufer vor sich hin. Doch die ersten Strahlen der Morgensonne kitzeln es gerade wach.

The shoreline at Horn has not yet awakened from its dreams. But the first rays of the morning sun will soon tickle it awake.

Nur früh am Morgen findet man auf der Terrasse dieses Seerestaurants in Gaienhofen noch so viel Platz und kann den Ausblick auf das gegenüberliegende Schweizer Ufer in Ruhe genießen.

Only early in the morning can one find so many vacant seats on the terrace of this lakeside restaurant in Gaienhofen, and enjoy in peace and quiet the view of the opposite Swiss shore.

Abendliche Stille kehrt am Untersee ein. Von diesem verlassenen Bootssteg in Hemmenhofen aus lässt sich der Sonnenuntergang ungestört erleben.

Evening calm returns to the Untersee. The sunset can be experienced with no disturbances from this deserted landing stage in Hemmenhofen.

Wangen. Das Schweizer Ufer ist zum Greifen nah – so nah, dass man ohne größere Mühe einfach in die Schweiz schwimmen könnte.

Wangen. The Swiss shore is almost near enough to touch – so near that it would be quite easy to swim over to Switzerland.

Der steile Schiener Berg durchzieht die Halbinsel Höri. Er besteht aus Schichten der Oberen Süßwassermolasse und gilt als wichtige Fundstätte für Fossilien.

The steep "Schiener Berg" traverses the Höri peninsula. It consists of strata built up during the upper Tertiary Period, which contain many fossils.

Öhningen ist der letzte deutsche Ort vor der Schweizer Grenze. Von hier aus führt ein beschaulicher Uferpfad in die Schweiz, und nur der Bundesadler auf dem Schild zeigt an, dass man soeben eine Staatsgrenze übertreten hat.

Öhningen is the last German village before the Swiss border. From here, a leisurely lakeside stroll leads into Switzerland, with only the German eagle on the signpost to indicate that a national border has just been crossed.

Bei Stein am Rhein verjüngt sich der Bodensee wieder zum Fluss Rhein. Umgeben von Weinbergen und überragt von der Burg Hohenklingen, ist dieses Schweizer Städtchen vor allem für seine schmucke Altstadt bekannt.

At Stein am Rhein, Lake Constance narrows and tapers again to become the river Rhein. Surrounded by vineyards and dominated by the "Burg Hohenklingen", this small Swiss town is best known for its neat old town.

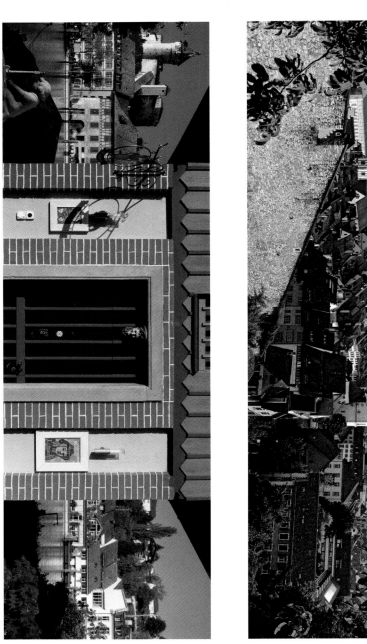

Schaffhausen hat nicht nur die berühmten Rheinfälle zu bieten, die mit einer Abflussmenge von rund 600000 Litern pro Sekunde die größten Wasserfälle Europas sind. Auch die Stadt selbst wartet mit zahlreichen Sehenswürdigkeiten auf, darunter das Schloss Laufen, das über den Rheinfällen thront, eine gut erhaltene Altstadt mit Münster und St. Johannturm und zahlreichen Beispielen traditioneller Schweizer Architektur, wie dem „Wöschhüsli" am Ufer des Rheins.

Schaffhausen boasts not only the famous Rhein Falls, which with a flow of 600,000 litres per second are the largest waterfalls in Europe. The town itself also has many sights to offer, such as the "Schloss Laufen" which towers up above the Rhein Falls, a well-preserved old town with Münster and the "St. Johannturm" and numerous examples of traditional Swiss architecture, such as the "Wöschhüsli" on the banks of the Rhein.

Über saftige grüne Wiesen hinweg fällt der Blick auf das kleine Örtchen Mammern, das schon in der Jungsteinzeit besiedelt war. Auch viele andere Uferdörfer am Schweizer Untersee bieten faszinierende Ausblicke. Wie etwa Berlingen, das vor allem durch den Kunstmaler Adolf Dietrich berühmt wurde, Steckborn, wo die Zinnen des alten Turmhofes schon von Weitem ins Auge fallen, oder Mannenbach, das vom benachbarten Arenberg aus gut zu sehen ist.

Passing over lush green meadows, the gaze falls on the tiny village of Mammern, which was already settled by Neolithic times. Many other lakeside villages on the Swiss Untersee also offer wonderful views, such as Berlingen, which became famous above all due to the painter Adolf Dietrich, Steckborn, where the battlements of the old "Turmhof" can be spotted far and wide, or Mannenbach, which can also be clearly seen from the neighbouring Arenberg.

Die Fachwerkfassaden von Ermatingen glänzen in der Morgensonne.

The half-timbered façades of Ermatingen gleam in the morning sun.

Bei Triboltingen stört nur wenig Bebauung den Blick auf das herbstlich gefärbte Bodenseeufer.

At Triboltingen there are only few buildings to impede the view of the Lake Constance shoreline in its autumn livery.

Ein Landesteg in Triboltingen im Licht des frühen Morgens. Im Hintergrund ist die Pappelallee der Insel Reichenau zu erkennen.

A landing stage at Triboltingen in the early morning light. The poplar avenue on the island of Reichenau can be made out in the background.

Gottlieben liegt am Ufer des Seerheins, der Ober- und Untersee verbindet. Auf der anderen, deutschen Seite beginnt das Naturschutzgebiet Wollmatinger Ried.

Gottlieben lies on the banks of the Seerhein, which connects the Obersee with the Untersee. On the other side, in Germany, lies the nature preservation area of the "Wollmatinger Ried."

OBERSEE

DAS „DREI-LÄNDER-MEER" THE "LAKE OF THREE COUNTRIES"

Lieblich blau oder bleiern grau oder giftig grün mit weißen Schaumkronen – der Obersee hat viele Gesichter. Sonne glitzert auf dem Wasser, die Wellen flüstern, Enten schnattern, dann scheint der See mit den Alpen zu flirten. Urplötzlich zieht ein Sturm heran, dann kann er wild werden. Seine Größe erlaubt hohe Wellen, die mit Wucht ans Ufer peitschen. Seine Weite – zwölf Kilometer sind es von Friedrichshafen nach Romanshorn, vierzehn nach Arbon – gibt dem See den Beinamen „Schwäbisches Meer". Im Osten hat das österreichische Vorarlberg mit Bregenz einen Anteil am See. „Drei-Länder-Meer" wäre der passende Name.

Soft blue or leaden grey, or bilious green with white horses – the "Obersee" has many faces. Sun glitters on the water, the waves whisper, ducks cackle, the lake appears to flirt with the Alps. Suddenly a storm approaches, and the lake can now become wild. Its size allows high waves, which lash the shore with force. Its expanse – twelve kilometres from Friedrichshafen to Romanshorn, and fourteen to Arbon – has given the lake its nickname of the "Swabian Sea". In the east, the Austrian Vorarlberg shares part of the shore, the "lake of three countries" would be the appropriate name.

Sonnenufer heißt die deutsche Seeseite, das Nordufer, zwischen Hagnau und Lindau. Ein Zwilling des Nordufers ist die Schweizer Seite nicht, denn es fehlt der überwältigende Blick auf den See mit dem Alpenpanorama dahinter. Die Schweizer müssen sich mit dem oberschwäbischen Hügelland als Kulisse für den See zufrieden geben. Dafür hat der Tourismus das Schweizer Ufer noch nicht überrannt. Die Strandbäder sind leerer, auf den Uferpromenaden flaniert man gemütlicher und in den Straßencafés findet sich leichter ein freier Platz als am Sonnenufer.

"Sonnenufer" (sunny bank) is the name of the German side of the lake, the northern shore, between Hagnau and Lindau. The Swiss side is not a twin of the northern shore, since it lacks the overwhelming view of the lake with the Alpine panorama behind it. The Swiss must be content with the Upper Swabian hill country as the backdrop to the lake. Tourism has therefore not yet overrun the Swiss shore of the lake. The beaches are less crowded, the promenades more pleasant for strolling, and in the street cafés, it is much easier to find a seat than on the northern side.

1855 kam die erste Schweizer Eisenbahn am Bodensee, in Romanshorn, an und verwandelte das alte Fischerdorf in einen bedeutenden Verkehrsknotenpunkt für den Fährverkehr. Früher wurden auch Eisenbahnwaggons mit den Fähren transportiert, heute sind es nur noch Straßenfahrzeuge. Vielleicht kam auch der Leipziger Schriftsteller Carl Sternheim mit der Fähre in Romanshorn an. Er ließ sich 1918 als Emigrant ein Dorf weiter, in Uttwil, nieder. Schnell war der Exzentriker dafür bekannt, bis in den frühen Morgen zu arbeiten. War er fertig mit seinem Tun, fing sein Nachbar, ein Zimmermann, singend an zu hobeln und zu sägen. Wütend habe Sternheim dann das Fenster aufgerissen und dem Nachbarn unter Beschimpfungen einige Franken vor die Füße geworfen, mit der Bitte, er möge aufhören. Regelmäßig habe sich der Zimmermann so ein Zubrot verdient.

The first Swiss railway line came to Lake Constance in 1855, at Romanshorn, turning the old fishing village into an important transport hub for the ferry traffic. In earlier times, railway carriages were also transported by the ferries, although today they carry only road vehicles. Perhaps the Leipzig author Carl Sternheim also arrived in Romanshorn by ferry. He settled in the area in 1918 as an emigrant, one village further along in Uttwil. The eccentric soon became known for his habit of working into the early hours. When he was finished with his labours, his

neighbour, a carpenter, began singing as he hammered and sawed away. Sternheim angrily threw open the window and threw a few francs at the feet of the carpenter, shouting at him and asking him to stop. The carpenter regularly earned a little extra pocket money in this way.

„Glücklicher Baum", Arbon felix, nannten die Römer das Städtchen am Nordufer. Arbon felix – das Tor zum eidgenössischen Obstgarten. Hügel, übersät mit Feldern und Obstbäumen. Arbon ist auch das Zentrum „Mostindiens", wie die Gegend spöttisch genannt wird. Apfelsaft, Apfelwein, Apfelchampagner und Apfelkuchen, alles dreht sich um Äpfel. Kein Wunder, denn im Thurgau wird ein Drittel aller in der Schweiz gewachsenen Äpfel geerntet. Die wirtschaftliche Blüte war früher eng mit der Maschinenbauindustrie verbunden: Bis in die achtziger Jahre produzierte Saurer, der größte Automobil- und Motorenhersteller der Schweiz, in Arbon Lastwagen.

"Happy tree", Arbon felix, was the name given by the Romans to the village on the northern shore. Arbon felix – the gateway to the market garden of Switzerland. Hills, studded with fields and fruit trees. Arbon is also the centre of "Mostindien" ("cider India"), as the region is derisively called. Apple juice, apple wine, apple champagne and apple tart, everything here revolves around apples. No wonder, because one third of all apples grown in Switzerland are harvested in Thurgau. Economic development was earlier closely associated with the engineering industry: until the 1980s, Saurer, the largest vehicle and engine manufacturer in Switzerland, produced commercial vehicles in Arbon.

Vom See profitierte die Stadt Rorschach schon früh und von ihrer Nähe zu St. Gallen. Getreide aus Oberschwaben wurde importiert, und von Rorschach aus nach St. Gallen oder weiter in die Schweiz transportiert. Stattliche Bürgerhäuser und das Kornhaus am Hafen, einer der schönsten Getreidespeicher der Schweiz, zeugen vom Reichtum vergangener Tage. Ein Spaziergang am Seeufer führt zu einer der schönsten alten Jugendstil-Badeanstalten am See. Im Sommer ist nicht nur das Bad einen Besuch wert, sondern auch das Sandskulpturenfestival im August. Um die Kunstwerke möglichst lange bewundern zu können, bedarf es eines trockenen Sommers.

The town of Rorschach benefited from the lake at an early stage, and from its closeness to St. Gallen. Linen and cotton goods were exported, and corn was imported from Upper Swabia, and transported from Rorschach to St. Gallen or further into Switzerland. Stately merchants' houses and the "Kornhaus" at the harbour, one of the most beautiful granaries in Switzerland, testify to the wealth of past times. A stroll along the lake shore leads to one of the most beautiful old art nouveau bathhouses on the lake. In summer, the baths are well worth a visit, together with the sand sculpture festival in August. In order to be able to admire these works of art for as long as possible, it needs a dry summer.

Direkt an der Mündung des Alten Rheins in den Bodensee liegt das Schweizer Fischerdorf Altenrhein. Die Hauptmenge des Rheinwassers fließt allerdings einige Kilometer östlich, auf österreichischem Gebiet durch einen Kanal in die Fußacher Bucht. Zwischen Altenrhein und dem Kanal liegt das Rheindelta, das größte Binnenseedelta Europas. Eine rund 2.000 Hektar große geschützte Landschaft aus Schilfröhricht, Feuchtwiesen und Auwäldern. Lebensraum, Brut- und Rastplatz für mehr als 330 seltene und bedrohte Vogelarten und weit über 500 Blütenpflanzen und Farne.

Right where the Alter Rhein flows into Lake Constance lies the Swiss fishing village of Altenrhein. Most of the water of the Rhein however flows a few kilometres to the east, on Austrian territory, through a canal into the bay at Fußach. Between Altenrhein and the canal lies the Rhein delta, the largest inland lake delta in Europe, a 5,000-acre protected landscape of reed beds, water meadows and alluvial forests. The habitat, breeding and resting ground of over 330 rare and endangered species of birds and well over 500 flowering plants and ferns.

Trotz seiner Kanalisation ist der Alpenrhein ein großer Wildbach geblieben, der enorme Sedimentmassen mit sich führt, die das Mündungsgebiet ständig verändern. So sind allein im 20. Jahrhundert mehr als zwei Quadratkilometer neue Landfläche entstanden. Seit den siebziger Jahren werden die Rheindämme weiter seewärts gestreckt, damit die Sedimente in tiefere Seebereiche gelangen und die Verlandung im Uferbereich gestoppt wird. Auf lange Sicht wird das aber nichts nützen, denn eines fernen Tages wird der Bodensee verlandet sein. *Despite its canalisation, the Alpenrhein has remained a great, wild torrent, carrying with it enormous masses of sediment, which continually change the shape of the estuary. More than two square kilometres of new land area were created in the 20th Century alone. Since the 1970s, the Rhein embankments have been extended further towards the lake, so that the sediments are deposited in deeper areas of the lake, stopping the creation of new land in the shore area. In the long term however this will be of no benefit, and at some time in the distant future, Lake Constance will be completely silted up.*

Ob es Bregenz, die älteste Stadt am See, dann noch geben wird? Bereits die Römer hatten in „Brigantium" ihr Verwaltungszentrum und einen Handelsstützpunkt eingerichtet. Den Römern folgten die Alamannen, die irischen Mönche und das Geschlecht der Grafen von Montfort, die im 16. Jahrhundert Bregenz an die Habsburger verkauften. Papierproduktion und Baumwollspinnerei entstehen im 19. Jahrhundert, Industrialisierung und Tourismus beginnen. *Will Bregenz, the oldest town on the lake, still be here then? The Romans established their administrative centre and a trading base here in "Brigantium". The Romans were followed by the Alemanni, the Irish monks and the dynasty of the counts of Montfort, who sold Bregenz to the Habsburgs in the 16th Century. Paper production and cotton spinning developed in the 19th Century, heralding the start of industrialisation and tourism.*

Der Martinsturm mit seiner mächtigen mit Schindeln bedeckten Zwiebelhaube, die um 1600 auf den Kornspeicher der ehemaligen Burganlage aufgesetzt worden ist, ist das Wahrzeichen der Altstadt, der Oberstadt. Ruhig, fast schon ein bisschen verschlafen geht es hier zu. Dagegen ist die Unterstadt das urbane Zentrum von Bregenz mit seiner Seefront, mit Cafés, Läden und Museen. Am Ufer entlang spaziert man durch Parkanlagen am postmodernen Hauptbahnhof vorbei zum Hafen. Der Blick fällt auf den Glaskubus des Kunsthauses, des Flaggschiffs der modernen Vorarlberger Architektur, das allerdings vom Schweizer Architekten Peter Zumthor entworfen worden ist. *The "Martinsturm" with its shingled, onion-shaped dome, which was built on to the granary of the former fortress complex around 1600, is the landmark of the old town, the upper town. The atmosphere here is calm, even a little sleepy. The lower town on the other hand is the urban centre of Bregenz with its lake front, cafés, shops and museums. Along the shore, people stroll through the parks past the post-modern main station to the harbour. The gaze falls on the glass cube of the "Kunsthaus", the flagship of modern Vorarlberg architecture, although it was designed by the Swiss architect Peter Zumthor.*

Schaut man von Lindau Richtung Bregenz, sieht der Pfänder keineswegs spektakulär aus. Obwohl mit 1.064 Metern der höchste Berg am See, kann es sein breiter Rücken an Schönheit und Pracht mit den schneebedeckten Alpenriesen am Horizont nicht aufnehmen. Wer ihn zu Fuß, mit dem Fahrrad oder bequem mit der Pfänderbahn besteigt, wird mit einem traumhaften Blick auf den Bodensee belohnt. Eine spiegelglatte blaue Ebene. Zur Linken breitet sich ein Häusermeer aus, das dicht besiedelte Rheintal mit Bregenz. Zur Rechten schiebt sich Lindau in den See hinein. *If one looks from Lindau in the direction of Bregenz, the Pfänder looks by no means spectacular. Although the highest mountain on the lake at 3,490 ft, its broad ridge cannot compare in beauty and splendour with the magnificent, snow-covered Alps on the horizon. Anyone climbing it on foot, by bicycle or more comfortably on the Pfänder mountain railway will be rewarded with a breathtaking view of Lake Constance. A blue plain, flat as a mirror. To the left, a sea of houses spreads out, the densely populated Rhein valley with Bregenz. To the right, Lindau thrusts itself into the lake.*

Der Geograf Sebastian Münster prägte 1544 den Beinamen „Schwäbisches Venedig" für die Stadt auf der Insel. „Glückseliges Lindau" seufzte der Schriftsteller Friedrich Hölderlin mehr als 200 Jahre später. Lindau, die malerische Stadt auf der Insel. Wie an zwei Tauen durch die Seebrücke und den Eisenbahndamm festgezurrt liegt die 68 Hektar große Insel im Bodensee. Das Wahrzeichen der Stadt ist die prächtige Hafeneinfahrt zwischen Leuchtturm und steinernem Löwen, der zum Glanze Bayerns errichtet worden ist – Lindau war 1805 ans Königreich Bayerns gefallen. *The geographer Sebastian Münster coined the nickname the "Venice of Swabia" for the town on the island in the year 1544. "Blissful Lindau" sighed the author Friedrich Hölderlin over 200 years later. Lindau, the picturesque town on the island. The 168-acre island lies in Lake Constance, as if moored by the two hawsers of the road bridge and railway embankment. The landmark of the town is the splendid harbour entrance between the lighthouse and the stone lion, which was placed here to the glory of Bavaria – Lindau became a possession of the kingdom of Bavaria in 1805.*

Überraschend spät ist die Insel im See besiedelt worden. Lange galt sie als zu sumpfig. Seine mittelalterliche Blüte erlebte Lindau durch die Linie des „Mailänder Boten", einer wichtigen Reiter- und Kutschenverbindung von Süddeutschland nach Norditalien, die in Lindau begann. Durch den Handel mit den oberitalienischen Städten war Lindau im 12. Jahrhundert eine der reichsten Städte Schwabens. Vom Reichtum erzählen die Prachtstraße, benannt nach Kaiser Maximilian, und das „Haus zum Cavazzen", das als das schönste Haus am See gilt. Mit der Eisenbahn begann 1853 der Massentourismus, von dem die denkmalgeschützte Stadt heute noch lebt. Am Ufer reifen Weintrauben, am Hafen tuten Schiffe, Enten quaken und ein mildes Lüftchen streicht über den See. Am schönsten ist ein Abend auf der Uferpromenade, wenn der Bodensee im Abendlicht glitzert, die Berge als Silhouette zu erahnen sind und der Hafen in einem Lichterkranz erstrahlt. Dann ist Lindau ganz südlicher Charme, „glückseliges Lindau". *The island in the lake was settled at a surprisingly late date. It was long considered to be too swampy. Lindau experienced its heyday in the Middle Ages due to the line of the "Mailänder Boten" ("Milan messengers"), an important horse and coach route from southern Germany to northern Italy, which began in Lindau. Thanks to the trade with the upper Italian cities, Lindau was one of the richest towns in Swabia in the 12th Century. The "Prachtstraße", named for Emperor Maximilian, and the "Haus zum Cavazzen", considered the most beautiful house on the lake, testify to the wealth of the town. The arrival of the railway in 1853 heralded the start of the mass tourism which is still the main source of income of this protected town today. Grapes ripen along the banks, ships toot in the harbour, ducks quack and a gentle breeze wafts over the lake. The most beautiful time is the evening on the shore promenade, when Lake Constance glitters in the evening light, the mountains can be made out in silhouette and the harbour shines out in a halo of light. Then Lindau is full of southern charm, "blissful Lindau".*

Wasserburg lag bis ins frühe 18. Jahrhundert auch auf einer Insel. Hier brachten sich schon im 10. Jahrhundert Mönche vor den Hunnen in Sicherheit. Weil die Fugger 1720 kein Geld für eine neue Zugbrücke zur Burg ausgeben wollten, füllten sie den Seegraben auf und machten Wasserburg zur Halbinsel.

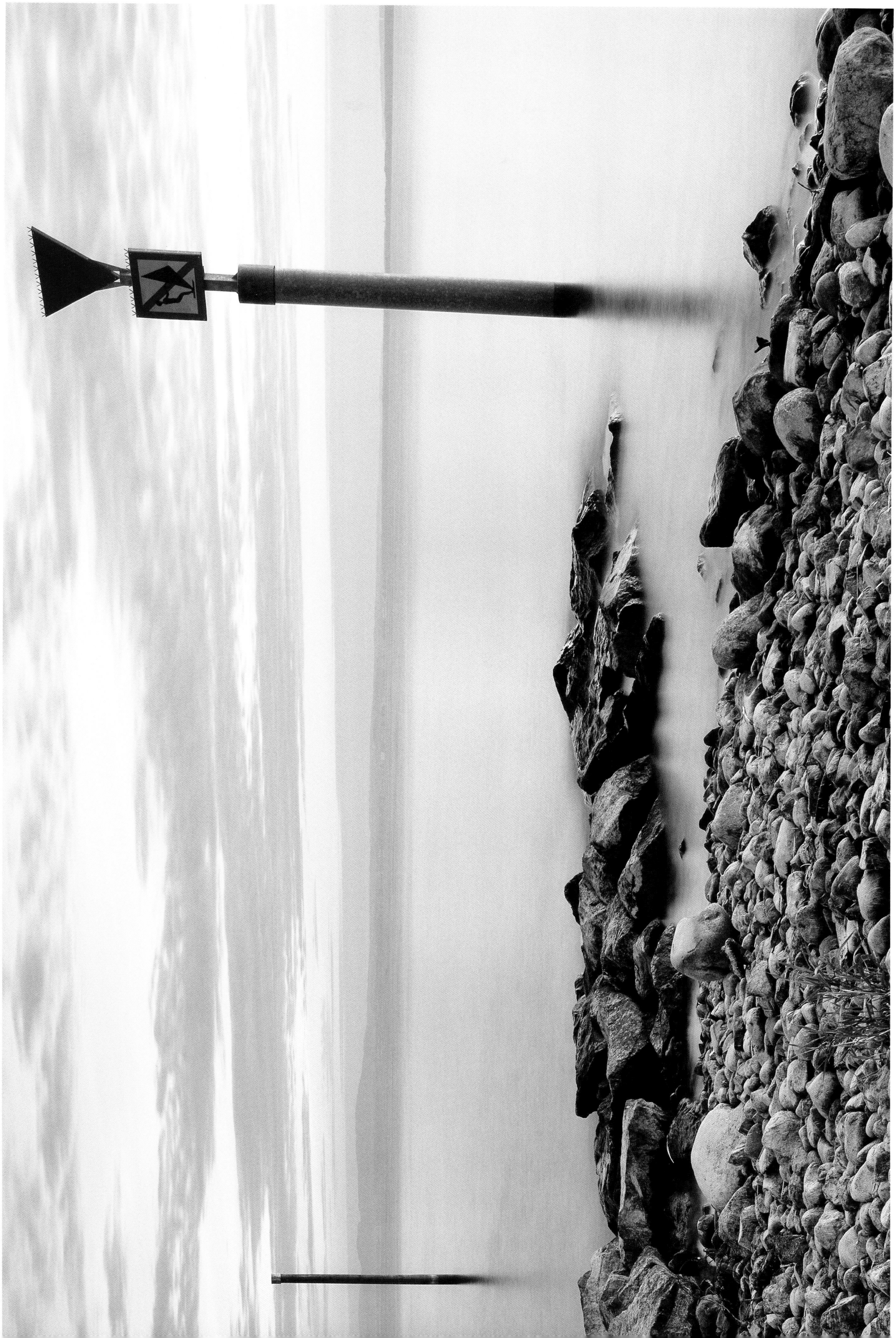

Das Kornhaus am Hafen ist eines der Wahrzeichen von Rorschach. Ähnliche Getreidespeicher lassen sich in fast allen Hafenstädten am Bodensee finden.

The "Kornhaus" on the harbour is one of the landmarks of Rorschach. Similar granaries can be found in almost all the harbour towns around Lake Constance.

122

Seezeichen bei Altenrhein. Hier mündet der Rhein in den Obersee, und entlang des Ufers lässt der Weidenbewuchs das ursprüngliche Aussehen des Flusses erahnen. Der größte Teil seiner Wassermassen wird inzwischen jedoch durch den schnurgeraden neuen Rheinkanal bei Fußach geleitet.

Navigation signs at Altenrhein. Here the Rhein flows into the Obersee, and along the bank, the meadow vegetation gives an idea of the original appearance of the river. Most of the outflowing volume of water is today directed through the dead straight, new Rhein Canal at Fußach.

124

Das Ostufer des Bodensees gehört zu Österreich. Die dichte Bebauung der Vorarlberger Landeshauptstadt Bregenz schmiegt sich entlang einer großen Bucht ans Wasser. Vom Hang oberhalb Lochaus aus schweift der Blick über die Bregenzer Innenstadt und die Rheinebene bis zu den Alpen.

The eastern shore of Lake Constance is Austrian territory. The dense development of the Vorarlberg state capital of Bregenz hugs the waterline around the fringe of a large bay. From the slope above Lochau, the gaze sweeps over the Bregenz inner city and the Rhein plain, and on to the Alps in the background.

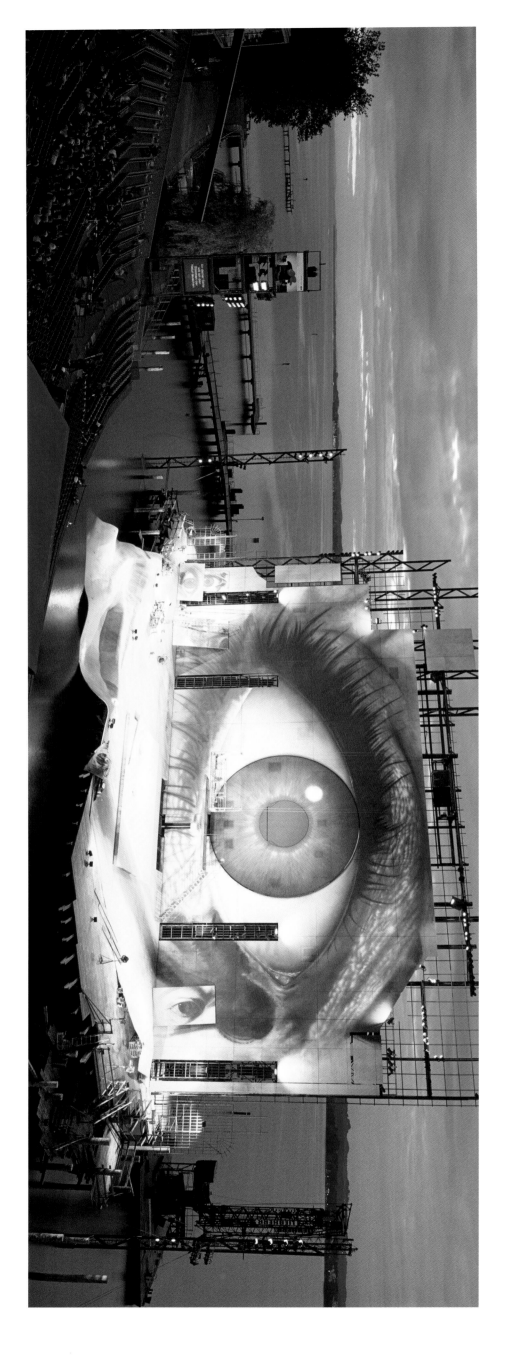

126

Die Bregenzer Festspiele mit der weltgrößten Seebühne, deren spektakulären Kulissen alle zwei Jahre gewechselt werden, ziehen ein internationales Publikum an. Es werden meist Opern oder Musicals aufgeführt, hier gerade die Oper „Tosca".

The Bregenz Festival Plays, with the world's largest lake stage, whose spectacular sets are changed every two years, attract an international audience. The pieces performed are usually operas or musicals, in this case the opera "Tosca".

The 3,490 ft. "Pfänder" is the local mountain of Bregenz. An Eldorado for hikers and skiers.

Der 1.064 m hohe Pfänder ist der Hausberg von Bregenz. Ein Eldorado für Wanderer und Skifahrer.

Die Inselsilhouette von Lindau zeichnet sich vor dem Abendhimmel ab. Der Leuchtturm an der Hafeneinfahrt, die beiden Kirchturmspitzen und das Spielkasino sind gut zu erkennen.

The island silhouette of Lindau is limned against the evening sky. The lighthouse at the harbour entrance, the two church spires and the casino can be seen clearly.

Langenargen. Herbststurm am Schloss Montfort.

Langenargen. Autumn storms over "Schloss Montfort".

The harbour mole of Langenargen in the dawn light.

Die Hafenmole von Langenargen im Morgenlicht.

Die Schlosskirche mit ihren hohen Kuppeltürmen aus Rorschacher Sandstein ist das Wahrzeichen der Stadt Friedrichshafen. Heute ist sie, genau wie das daneben liegende Schloss selbst, im Besitz des Herzogs von Württemberg.

The "Schlosskirche" with its high, domed spires of Rorschach sandstone is the landmark of the town of Friedrichshafen. Today, both it and the adjoining castle belong to the Duchy of Württemberg.

Vom Aussichtsturm an der Hafenmole hinunter hat man einen großartigen Blick auf die Häfler Innenstadt. Noch herrscht Ruhe entlang der Promenade, gerade erst ist die Sonne aufgegangen.

The observation tower on the harbour mole affords a magnificent view over the Häfle town centre. Calm still reigns along the promenade just after sun-up.

Der Nebel an Friedrichshafens Hafeneinfahrt beginnt sich zu lichten und gibt zögerlich den Blick auf den Molenturm frei. Schon bald wird hier alles in den Winterschlaf sinken.

The mist cloaking Friedrichshafen's harbour entrance begins to lift, gradually revealing the view of the mole tower. Soon everything here will fall into its winter sleep.

148

Die Überreste einer verfallenen Mole bei Manzell vor der grandiosen Kulisse des Säntismassivs im Sonnenuntergang.

The remains of a derelict mole at Manzell against the magnificent backdrop of the Säntis massif at sundown.

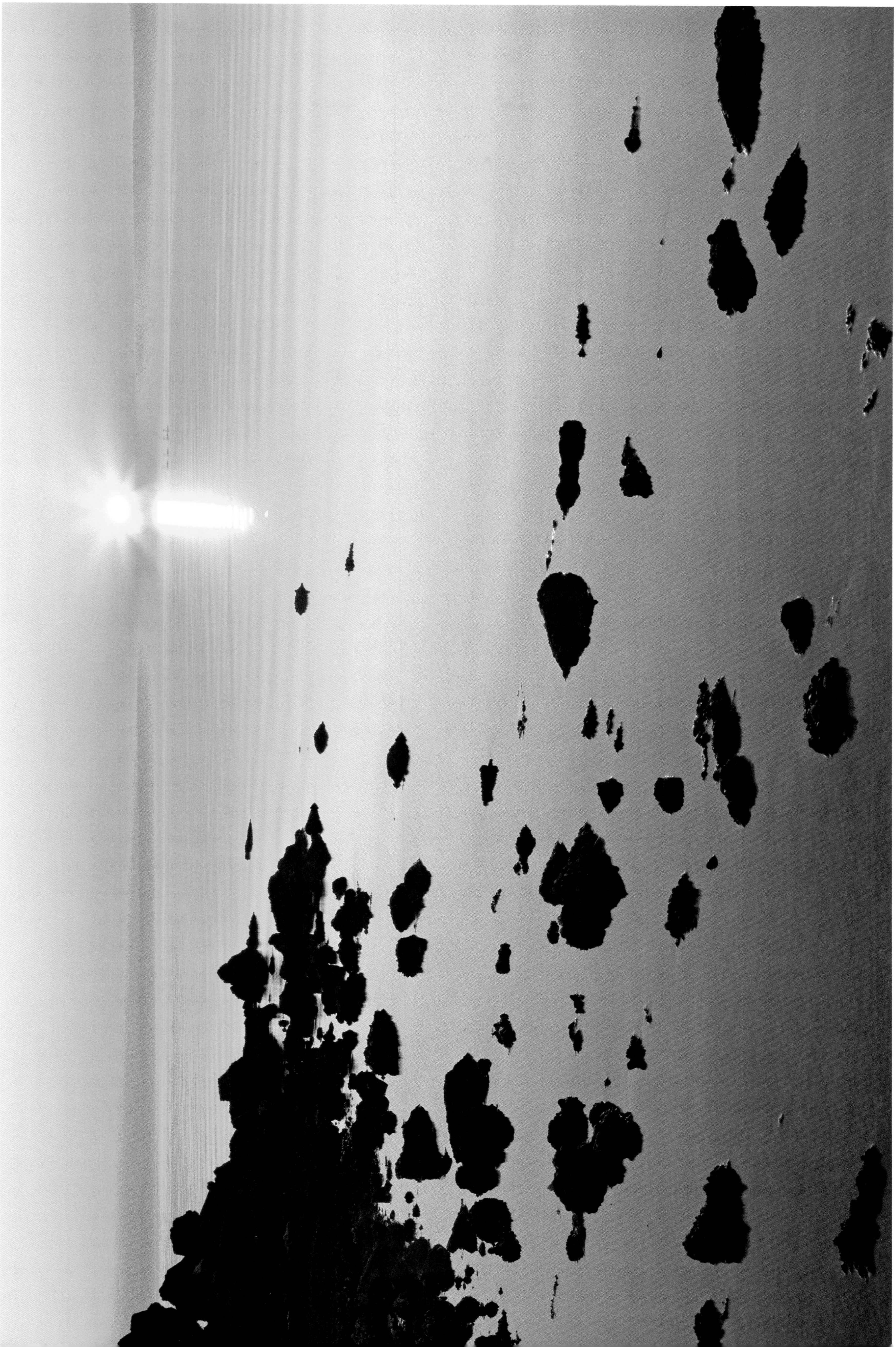

Nur wenigen Einheimischen bekannt ist die Dornier-Mole vor Immenstaad. Früher wurden auf diesen kleinen Inseln Torpedos getestet, heute sind sie wichtige Vogelbrutgebiete.

The Dornier mole near Immenstaad is known only to a few locals. In earlier times, torpedoes were tested on this small island, while today it is an important breeding ground for birds.

Vor der Immenstaader Schiffslände liegt die „Lädine" vor Anker. Sie ist ein Nachbau der traditionellen Lastensegler, die jahrhundertelang den Bodensee befahren haben.

The "Lädine" lies at anchor beside the Immenstaad landing stage. She is a reproduction of the traditional cargo boats which plied Lake Constance for centuries.

Im Abendlicht ziehen dunkle Herbstwolken über die Immenstaader Schiffsanlegestelle.
Dark autumn clouds gather over the Immenstaad landing stage in the evening light.

Regenschleier über dem See bei Immenstaad.

Misty rain over the lake near Immenstaad.

Hagnau in der Abenddämmerung. Von der „Wilhelmshöhe" hinab bietet sich vor allem bei Föhn eine beeindruckende Aussicht auf die Alpenkette und auf das gegenüberliegende Seeufer.

Hagnau at twilight. The „Wilhelmshöhe" offers an impressive view of the Alps and the opposite shore of the lake, particularly when the Föhn wind is blowing.

ANMERKUNGEN DES FOTOGRAFEN NOTES BY THE PHOTOGRAPHER

© Edmund Möhrle, Friedrichshafen

„Ihr wohnt ja hier im Paradies!" – nicht nur Urlauber, Kurgäste und andere Besucher, die den Bodensee zum ersten Mal besuchen, geraten oft ins Schwärmen. Auch langjährige Anwohner erliegen immer wieder aufs Neue der Faszination dieser Landschaft und staunen über die Wandlungsfähigkeit des Sees: Täglich, manchmal stündlich zeigt er ein anderes Gesicht, offenbart neue Farb- und Wetterstimmungen. Bei meiner Arbeit als Fotograf erlebe ich ein uns andere Mal, dass selbst altbekannte Motive je nach Jahreszeit, Licht und Perspektive neue, außergewöhnliche Stimmungen hervorzaubern. Streuobstwiesen am Ufer lassen ein Meer weißer Blüten im Morgensonnenschein erstrahlen, vor der imposanten Alpensilhouette ziehen Segelboote dahin, Steine am Ufer bewegen sich im leisen Spiel auflaufender Wellen, während sich im Hintergrund vom Hegau her eine sommerliche Gewitterfront nähert oder blutrote Föhnwolken das Licht der untergehenden Sonne reflektieren. Eingebettet in diese Naturschauspiele liegen Kirchen und Schlösser aus alten Zeiten, malerisch in der Hügellandschaft verteilte Dörfchen. Alles hier atmet Frieden, Beschaulichkeit, Naturverbundenheit und Geschichte.

"Here you live in paradise!" – it is not only holidaymakers, spa patients and other visitors coming to Lake Constance for the first time who are often enchanted by it. Even those who have lived here for many years repeatedly succumb to the fascination of this landscape and are amazed at the changing appearance of the lake: daily, sometimes hourly, it shows a new face, revealing new shades of colour and temperaments of weather. In my work as a photographer, I experience time and again that even well-known motifs can conjure up new and unusual moods, depending on the season of the year, the light and the perspective. Meadows scattered with fruit trees along the shore make a sea of white blossoms shine out in the morning sun, sailing boats ply the gentle waves against the imposing silhouette of the Alps, pebbles on the shore move in the quiet play of the lapping waves, while in the background, from Hegau, a summer weather front approaches or blood-red Föhn clouds reflect the light of the setting sun. Embedded in this theatre of nature lie churches and castles from times long past, and villages dotted picturesquely amongst the rolling landscape. Everything here breathes peace, tranquillity, closeness to nature and a sense of history.

Ein Menschenleben würde nicht ausreichen, um all die Motive fotografisch umzusetzen, zu denen der Bodensee mich inspiriert. Ich kann nur versuchen, jeder Fotosaison ein paar neue Besonderheiten abzuringen. Mein Blick wandert durchs Fenster, ich beobachte Himmel und Wolken und ziehe los, sobald sich draußen etwas Ungewöhnliches abzeichnet. Seit zwei Kinder zu unserer Familie gehören, sind spontane Fotoexkursionen etwas seltener geworden; die Liebe zum See und der Wunsch, noch möglichst viele Bildträume umzusetzen, haben mich jedoch nicht verlassen.

A whole life would not be long enough to capture in pictures all the motifs to which Lake Constance inspires me. I can only try to wring from every photo season a few new special images. My gaze wanders to the window, I watch the sky and the clouds, and head out as soon as anything unusual appears to be happening outside. Since our family has come to include two children, spontaneous photography excursions have become somewhat less frequent; but I have not lost my love of the lake, or the desire to realise as many as possible of my photographic dreams.

Doch als einheimischer „Seehas", zumal als Landschaftsfotograf, muss ich oft auch Risse und Widersprüche im Erscheinungsbild dieser Landschaft wahrnehmen. Vielleicht werden mir durch meinen Beruf die umwälzenden Veränderungen der Landschaft auch nur schneller und deutlicher bewusst als Anderen und sie stimmen mich nachdenklich. Wo sich im letzten Jahr noch unberührte Streuobstwiesen vor meiner Kamera entfalteten, tauchen nun bereits Baukräne am Horizont auf, Obstplantagen weichen Stadtrandparkplätzen, die Innenstädte werden „nachverdichtet" auf Kosten der Grünflächen zwischen den Gebäuden, die letzten Seegrundstücke werden erschlossen, für teures Geld an private Investoren vergeben und dadurch für die Öffentlichkeit unzugänglich. Eine über Jahrhunderte, ja, Jahrtausende gewachsene Natur- und Kulturlandschaft hat sich zu Lebzeiten einer Generation gravierender geändert als im gesamten Lauf ihrer Geschichte zuvor. Obwohl die euphorischen Äußerungen der Besucher nach wie vor berechtigt sind und wir ein Glückslos gezogen haben mit unserer Heimat hier am südlichsten Zipfel Deutschlands, gilt es dennoch, die Kleinode dieser unvergleichlichen Landschaft nicht nur auf Fotos sondern auch in der Wirklichkeit zu erhalten.

But as a native lake-lover, and especially a landscape photographer, I am often forced to take note of cracks and contradictions in the appearance of this apparently so perfect holiday environment. Due to my profession, the sweeping changes of the landscape perhaps become apparent to me more quickly and clearly than to others, putting me in a pensive mood. Where last year unspoilt meadows dotted with fruit trees spread out in front of my camera, construction cranes now appear on the horizon, fruit plantations give way to suburban parking areas, the town centres are becoming "re-compressed" at the cost of the green areas between the buildings; the last properties around the lake are being developed, sold at high prices to private investors and therefore no longer accessible to the public. A natural and cultural landscape which has grown up over centuries, even millennia, has within the lifetime of a single generation changed more thoroughly than in the course of its complete past history. Although the euphoric utterances of visitors are still justified, and we have hit the jackpot with our home here at the southernmost tip of Germany, the beauty spots of this incomparable landscape must be preserved not only in photographs, but also in reality.

Dennoch begreife ich es als Privileg, die Faszination dieser Landschaft in Bilder umzusetzen und damit für die Ewigkeit zu bewahren. In diesem Sinne weist meine Arbeit dokumentarische Züge auf, allerdings charakterisiert durch eine selbst gewählte Einseitigkeit, denn ich strebe danach, die Wirklichkeit stets nur dann einzufangen, wenn sie am schönsten ist.

Nevertheless, I still consider it a privilege to be able to record the fascination of this landscape in pictures, and thereby preserve it for posterity. In this sense, my work is of a documentary nature, although characterised by a deliberate bias, because I strive to capture the reality only when it is at its most beautiful.

Seit vielen Jahren hat sich die Panoramakamera als das Werkzeug erwiesen, das dafür am besten geeignet ist. Zumindest ansatzweise kann sie den wirklichen Eindruck des Betrachters vor Ort festhalten, ohne auf einen unrealistisch großen Bildwinkel oder verzerrende Optik zurückzugreifen. Die Suche nach einer fotografischen Technik, die das wiedergeben kann, was das menschliche Auge erblickt, musste mich zur Panoramakamera führen, und es war eine Fuji GX617, für die ich mich vor langer Zeit entschieden habe. Noch immer ist sie die Kamera, mit der ich am liebsten unterwegs bin, auch wenn sie jetzt nicht mehr gebaut wird und sich mein Bildarchiv in den letzten Jahren durch hochauflösende, digital erstellte Panoramen erweitert hat. Die Vorzüge der Digitalfotografie nutze ich oft und gerne, aber sie stößt an ihre Grenzen, wenn sich im Motiv Dinge bewegen. Vor allem jedoch vermisse ich beim digitalen Fotografieren jenen Anflug von Weihnachtsstimmung, der aufkommt, wenn die gerade aus dem Labor gelieferten, 17 cm großen Diaoriginale auf dem Leuchttisch liegen und ein paar besonders gelungene Aufnahmen dabei sind. *For many years, the panoramic camera has proven to be the tool most suitable for this purpose. To some extent at least, it can replicate the actual impression of the observer on the spot, without having to resort to an unrealistically wide viewing angle or distorting visual effect. The search for a photographic technique which could reproduce what the human eye perceives inevitably led me to the panoramic camera, and it was a Fuji GX617 which I decided on long ago. This is still the camera I prefer to use on my travels, even if it is no longer in production, and my photography archive has been enlarged over recent years with the aid of high-resolution, digitally produced panoramas.* Ich use the advantages of digital photography often and gladly, but it comes up against its limits when things are moving in the picture. Above all however, with digital photography, I miss that sense of Christmas spirit which is stirred when the 17 cm large diapositive originals lie on the light-box, fresh from the laboratory, with a few particularly successful images amongst them.

Die fotografische Reise dieses Bildbandes folgt der Uferlinie des Sees. Sie soll einen Eindruck vermitteln von der Vielfalt unserer Bodenseelandschaft, in der sich Vergangenheit und Gegenwart die Hand reichen. Es ist mir jedoch auch ein persönliches Anliegen, auf die Gefährdung dieses noch weitgehend heilen kleinen Kosmos hinzuweisen. Gehen wir behutsam und dankbar mit ihm um! *The photographic journey of this illustrated volume follows the shoreline of the lake. It is intended to give an impression of the variety of our Lake Constance landscape, in which past and present come together. It is however also my personal concern to point out the dangers threatening this still largely unspoilt microcosm. Let us look after it with care and gratitude!*

Überlingen, September 2009

Holger Spiering

Für unsere Kinder Muenda und Mailin, die mich so oft entbehren müssen, weil ich zum Fotografieren unterwegs bin. Ich wünsche Euch beiden, dass auch Ihr eines Tages unsere herrliche Landschaft in ihrer Ursprünglichkeit genießen dürft, und dass Ihr mithelfen könnt, dieses wertvolle Erbe zu bewahren. *For our children Muenda and Mailin, who miss me so often because I am away taking photographs. I hope that you too can both one day enjoy our magnificent landscape in all its natural beauty, and that you can help to preserve this precious heritage.*

9000 – 5500 v. Chr. (BC): Steinzeitfunde belegen eine erste Besiedlung. *Stone Age findings confirm the earliest settlement.*

ab 4000 v. Chr. (from 4000 BC): Die Pfahlbauten entstehen. *The pile constructions are built.*

15 v. Chr. (15 BC): Die Römer besiegen die Kelten und beherrschen den Bodenseeraum. Bregenz, Arbon und Konstanz werden gegründet. 395 n. Chr. endet die Römerherrschaft, die Alamannen besiedeln nun das Land um den Bodensee. *The Romans conquer the Celts and control the Lake Constance region. Bregenz, Arbon and Konstanz are founded. 395 AD – Roman rule comes to an end, and the Alemanni now settle the land around Lake Constance.*

Um 550 (Around 550 AD): Das Bistum Konstanz wird gegründet. *The Bishopric of Konstanz is founded.*

8. Jahrhundert (8th Century): Klöster werden gegründet, beispielsweise St. Gallen (um 720) und Reichenau (724). Die fränkischen Könige wohnen ab 746 bei ihren Aufenthalten am Bodensee in der karolingischen Pfalz Bodman. *Monasteries are founded, such as those at St. Gallen (around 720) and Reichenau (724). From 746, the Frankish Kings reside in the Carolingian palatinate of Bodman during their stays at Lake Constance.*

Um 610 (Around 610 AD): Die Zeit der Wandermönche – Kolumban und Gallus, zwei irische Wandermönche, christianisieren die heidnische Bevölkerung. Gallus gründet ein Bethaus im Steinachtal. *The time of the itinerant monks – Columba and Gallus, two itinerant Irish monks, Christianise the heathen population. Gallus builds a prayer house in the Steinach valley.*

12. Jahrhundert (12th Century): Zisterzienser gründen 1134 das Kloster Salem. Friedrich Barbarossa hält einen Reichstag in Konstanz ab. Mit dem Frieden von Konstanz (1183) beendet Barbarossa den Krieg der Staufer gegen die oberitalienischen Städte. *Cistercians found the monastery of Salem in 1134. Friedrich Barbarossa holds an Imperial Diet in Konstanz. With the Peace of Konstanz (1183), Barbarossa ends the war of the "Staufer" against the upper Italian cities.*

1273: Der Niedergang der Staufer, die Habsburger dringen zum Bodensee vor, und Rudolf I. von Habsburg wird deutscher König. Teile des Bodensees kommen zu Vorderösterreich. *The downfall of the Staufer, the Habsburgs advance to Lake Constance, and Rudolf I of Habsburg becomes the German King. Parts of Lake Constance go to the Austrian Forelands.*

1414 – 1418: Beim Konzil in Konstanz werden Papst Martin V. gewählt und der Reformator Jan Hus als Ketzer verbrannt. *At the Council of Constance, Pope Martin V is elected, and the reformer Jan Hus burnt at the stake for heresy.*

1499: Die Truppen des Schwäbischen Bundes unterliegen im Schwabenkrieg. Der Thurgau kommt zur Eidgenossenschaft, und Konstanz wird Grenzstadt. *The forces of the Swabian League are defeated in the Swabian War. Thurgau passes to the Swiss Federation, and Konstanz becomes a border city.*

1521: Reformation in Konstanz, später auch in St. Gallen und Schaffhausen, die ländlichen Gebiete bleiben katholisch. 1547 wird auch Konstanz wieder katholisch. *Reformation in Konstanz, and later also in St. Gallen and Schaffhausen, the rural areas remain Catholic, and in 1547 Konstanz returns to Catholicism.*

1618–1648: Im Dreißigjährigen Krieg besetzen schwedische Gruppen die Mainau und Bregenz. In der ganzen Region, vor allem aber am Nordufer, kommt es zu großen Zerstörungen, denen der wirtschaftliche Niedergang folgt. *In the Thirty Years War, Swedish troops occupy Mainau and Bregenz. Great destruction is caused throughout the whole region, particularly on the northern shore, followed by the collapse of the economy.*

1803: Während der Säkularisierung werden alle Klöster aufgelöst. *All the monasteries are dissolved during secularisation.*

1848: Friedrich Hecker ruft in Konstanz die Deutsche Republik aus. *Friedrich Hecker proclaims the German Republic in Konstanz.*

1900: Am 1. Juli steigt der erste Zeppelin in Friedrichshafen auf. *The first Zeppelin is launched from Friedrichshafen on 1st July.*

1939 – 1945: Im Zweiten Weltkrieg wird der schweizerische Bodenseeraum Zuflucht für viele Verfolgte. Auf der anderen Seite – in Friedrichshafen, das weitgehend durch Luftangriffe zerstört wird – entsteht ein Außenlager des Konzentrationslagers Dachau. *In the Second World War, the Swiss part of Lake Constance becomes the destination for many refugees. On the other side, in Friedrichshafen, which is largely destroyed by bombing raids, an annex of the Dachau concentration camp is built.*

1966: Gründung der Reform-Universität auf dem Gießberg in Konstanz. *Foundation of the Reform University in Konstanz.*

2000: Die Reichenau wird UNESCO-Weltkulturerbe. *The island of Reichenau becomes a UNESCO world cultural heritage site.*